MEMORIES —

THE "SHOW-BIZ" PART OF MY LIFE

A WALT DISNEY CARTOON OF
PETER USTINOV AS "BLACKBEARD'S GHOST" &
HANK JONES AS "GUDGER LARKIN"

MEMORIES —

THE "SHOW-BIZ" PART OF MY LIFE

By
Hank Jones

PENOBSCOT PRESS

International Standard Book Number 0-89725-777-4
Library of Congress Control Number 2006903387

First Printing May 2006

This book is available from:
Henry Z Jones, Jr.
PO Box 261388
San Diego, CA 92196-1388
www.hankjones.com

*FOR DEAN KAY THOMPSON &
LARRY RAY HAYES –*

WITHOUT WHOM ...

FOR MY FRIENDS & FAMILY

Every so often at one of my genealogical seminars around the country, someone would saunter over to my book table and ask me a question, not about family history research, but about my days back in the stone age when I was in show business. With the advent of cable television and DVDs, my old movies and television shows that I thought were long forgotten have been resurrected and broadcast to a new and eager audience. Every old program and show now has its own dedicated group of buffs and fans who know every episode by heart and can spout off the names of cast and crew alike. I've had complete strangers come up to me and recite the lines I had in a film or TV program verbatim when I never even knew the dialogue myself in the first place.

"What was it really like back then?", "What was 'so-and-so' like off-camera?", "How did they manage to do THAT?" are all familiar questions I get to this day. I always say in my family history talks that if your ancestor happened to leave a journal or a diary of his or her life way back when, then you've been living a clean life and have been blessed: because genealogy when done correctly, puts flesh and blood on the skeleton of names and dates and makes our forbears come alive again. So I decided to "practice what I preach:" to write down for my daughter Amanda, and myself too, my reminiscences of my show-biz days back when the dinosaurs roamed – thus this short book.

I've always been a *people*-person. Some of the names on these pages you'll readily remember; others, sadly, are now pretty well forgotten. Many individuals I knew very well; others I only interacted with briefly. You'll find a lot of trivia here; but as someone once told me, "Hank – you ARE trivia!" Hopefully at least you'll get a *feel* for my friends and coworkers as they flitted in and out of my life in the entertainment business. At the time, they all were important: we were all on the same boat, just struggling to survive in a tough business. But now in hindsight, I realize we truly were a part of a magical time in

America – they were indeed "Happy Days," just like the title of the TV show.

So here goes. Come along with me on my somewhat wacky journey. You'll meet some intriguing people, I guarantee you that. Even though it's sometimes known for being rough and tough, I hope you'll see that Hollywood DOES have a heart.

Show business has brought forth some great characters, and some of the stories about them are pretty wild. I love to collect them. To start things off, here are a few somewhat off-the-wall anecdotes that always have made me smile:

My buddy John Craig supposedly was drafted to pick up a grieving Boris Karloff, the movie's immortal "Frankenstein," and take him to Bela Lugosi's funeral. Bela had a sad end, and the last twenty years of his life was spent trying to kick a stubborn drug-habit. Poor Boris mourned his departed friend greatly, and the only way to soften his pain was by imbibing in a series of strong drinks prior to the service. By the time John arrived to take Boris to the funeral, Mr. Karloff was totally schnockered. When they got to the church, Boris stumbled out of the car and reeled up the center aisle until he reached Bela's coffin. There was Lugosi, hair slicked back, white-faced, and all-dressed-up in his Dracula costume complete with his black cape. Boris Karloff looked down at the body, stared at his late friend, and bellowed loudly for all in the church to hear, "Bela - quit f**king around and get out of that coffin!"

Sir Ralph Richardson, the distinguished British actor so memorable in "The Heiress" and "Dr. Zhivago" was known for being quite a character. Although he was one of the greatest thespians of his generation along with Laurence Olivier and John Gielgud, he was known for tweaking the establishment. He would zig and zag all over London on his souped-up motor bike wearing his plaid cap and leather jacket which gave rise to many speeding tickets. Once when he was found by police walking very slowly along the gutter of an Oxford street, Sir Ralph explained he was taking his pet mouse for a stroll. My favorite yarn about the great actor was when he was at a formal banquet in Hollywood and toasts were being made to distinguished personages around the table. When it finally became Sir Ralph Richardson's turn to make his toast, he stood up, and instead of raising his glass to someone there at the dinner, said instead, "To Jesus Christ: What a *splendid* chap!"

A young reporter was trying to put together a newspaper story on important movie stars of the day. He especially wanted to include Cary Grant in the article. He couldn't get an exact birth-date for the actor so, in order to obtain the correct information, sent a wire to the star that said in telegraphese, "How old Cary Grant?" The star replied via return telegram, "Old Cary Grant fine. How you?"

George Burns and Gracie Allen were one of Hollywood's longest lasting and most devoted couples. Far from being the scatterbrain she portrayed on the screen, Gracie was an intelligent, sensitive woman, deeply devoted to her husband and even willing to forgive him his only brief dalliance outside their marriage. After she had passed away, George told the story of his one slip in fidelity – a meaningless one-night-stand with a chorus girl he met on the road, Afterwards, Burns was consumed with guilt that overwhelmed him because the affair occurred in the wake of a very rare serious argument between the two over a pricey centerpiece that Gracie coveted. To assuage his guilt, George bought her the centerpiece anyway. Months later, he noted that he heard Gracie tell a friend, "Gee, I wish George would cheat on me again. I could use a new centerpiece."

Brian Wilson, founder and creative genius behind "The Beach Boys," was on "Larry King Live" being interviewed in depth by the talk-show host. He went into great detail about his past troubles with drugs, the rock and roll fast lane, and his battle with mental illness over many years. Over most of the show Wilson went on and on talking about the depths of his descent into near madness. At the end of the program, King asked Brian, "With all that's happened to you in your life, do you have any regrets?" Wilson responded, "Yeah – I'd like to change the tempo of the drums on 'California Girls.'"

Bob Crosby became a good friend of writer Hal Kanter during the war years and told Hal that he was terribly bummed out trying to get ahead as a singer while living in the shadow of his brother Bing. One night when he was on the road Bob picked up a girl and took her back to his room. They got *very* well acquainted in a short period of time, things reached a fever pitch, and at the climactic moment of their lovemaking the girl yelled out, "Are Bing's eyes as blue in person as they are on the screen?"

Walter Matthau and Jack Lemmon were good and devoted real-life friends off camera. Once when filming one of their "Grumpy Old Men" movies, Walter had to shoot a scene perched on a high riser some fifteen feet over the soundstage floor. Just before the cameras rolled, he lost his footing and fell crashing to concrete floor below. Lemmon, who had seen the accident, was deeply concerned and rushed immediately over to his pal who lay unconscious at the bottom of the riser. Jack was beside himself, not knowing what to do and thought that perhaps his friend was dead. To do at least something to help, he took off his coat and gently put it under Matthau's head. He leaned over his friend and urgently inquired, "Walter, are you *comfortable*?" Walter Matthau slowly opened his eyes and looked up and said, "I make a living."

The "Come up and see me sometime" girl Mae West made movies well into her 80s, but in her last years just couldn't remember her lines. It was costing Paramount millions due to her memory lapses. So in desperation, the director had the brilliant idea of having the script girl feed Miss West her dialogue through a hidden earpiece worn under the star's big blonde wig. Everything was going along fine until one fateful day when the KMPC radio traffic helicopter happened to fly right over the studio. Miss West was in the middle of filming an important scene with her much-younger hunk of a boyfriend. Somehow the wires to her earpiece got crossed between the script girl and the helicopter, and Mae West uttered the now-immortal lines, "I love you Big Boy - and traffic is backed up on the 101 all the way to La Brea Avenue."

Merv Griffin tells a great story about Tallulah Bankhead, the hard-living, hard-drinking actress whose escapades were legendary throughout Hollywood. It happened over Christmas one year outside one of the major department stores. Tallulah was walking past the store, and one of the seasonal Salvation Army workers, a young girl, was shaking a tambourine to get people's attention for a donation. Tallulah stopped, studied the girl for moment, and then reached in purse and gave her a hundred dollar bill. Recognizing her, the stunned girl could only say, "Oh Miss Bankhead, thank you *so* much!" "That's all right, Dahling," said Tallulah gravely. "I know it's been a *terrible* year for you Spanish dancers."

Ego can sometimes get in the way of talent. There was once a legendary vaudevillian named Nora Bayes who worked in an act with her husband. She insisted on the marquee billing:

"Nora Bayes! Assisted and Admired by Jack Norworth"

In keeping with this, my comedy-writer friend Paul Pumpian was at a party with TV writer and jack-of-all-trades Stanley Ralph Ross. Stan was a hustling go-getter and a master at the art of self-promotion. Nobody loved Stan more than Stan. He had no fear and could out-talk and out-hype anybody. At the gathering, they gravitated towards each other and when Stanley Ralph found out Paul was also a writer he went on and on (and on) for about fifteen minutes detailing his latest triumphs in the business, all the important people he knew, all the scripts he sold, *ad infinitum*. Every so often Stanley Ralph would ask, "How about you?" to which Paul would reply, "Well I …" and off Stan would go again on another tirade, bragging away. Finally, it appeared he had at long last finished with his litany of accomplishments. Paul heaved a sigh of relief that his ordeal was over. But no - not quite: Stanley Ralph Ross then puffed himself up and looked down at the diminutive Paul and asked him, "How tall are you?" Paul replied, "Why I'm 5' 6." Drawing himself up to his full height, Stanley Ralph Ross proudly proclaimed, as if he had done it all himself, "*I'M* 6 FOOT 7!"

Paul has another good story to tell - this time, a heartwarming one: he was in charge of publicity for Gene Norman's old "Crescendo" nightclub on Sunset Strip years ago. One of the acts he had to promote was a new headliner, Allan Sherman, who had a very big comedy record at the time "Hello Mudda – Hello Fadda." The owners of the club needed someone VERY special to introduce Allan to the huge crowd that was expected at his opening, and at first no one could come up with a big enough name to do the job. But Allan said not to worry – that he had a big fan who had volunteered to introduce him. He told Gene Norman, the owner, who it was. Norman was overjoyed; but they kept the identity of the mystery-man a secret to everyone else, even Paul. The big night of Allan Sherman's debut finally arrived and the room was packed with an audience ready to be entertained. The lights dimmed and the crowd quieted down. Then a small, balding Jewish man got up from his table and slowly walked to the microphone. Dressed in a conservative dark suit, he looked like someone's accountant –

nobody could figure out who this guy was. There was total silence as the audience leaned forward to hear him. The little man cleared his throat and softly said, "Good evening, ladies and gentlemen – my name is Harpo Marx." With that, the entire nightclub burst into an ovation that lasted for a full five minutes – screaming, shouting, pounding the tables in appreciation for the man at the mike. Paul said he never before or since has witnessed an audience response of that magnitude.

    HARPO <u>TALKED</u>!

BEGINNINGS

I started young. I guess I was a weird kid. I must have been all of five years old when I made a microphone out of tinker-toys and pretended I was broadcasting a radio show from my bedroom. I was weaned on those old kids' radio shows like "Big John and Sparky," with Gil Hooey Mahoney and his Leprechaun Marching Band, and "The Comic-Weekly Man," the theme of which was:

> "Oh I'm the Comic Weekly Man, the jolly Comic
> Weekly Man, and I'm here to read the funnies for
> you happy boys and honeys".

And, of course, "The Lone Ranger," "The Shadow," "Sergeant Preston of the Yukon" (and his wonder-dog, "Yukon King"), and the soaps like "Young Widder Brown," "Mary Noble - Backstage Wife," and "Lorenzo Jones and his wife Belle" were staples around the Jones household.

I traveled around the country on trips with my folks from an early age. One of my youthful treats was when they took me to see actual broadcasts of my favorite radio programs. We took a big trip when I was nine years old. In New York City, we enjoyed listening to Vincent Lopez and his Orchestra play society dance tunes at the Hotel Taft Grill ("Lopez speaking" was his opening greeting on the air). In Chicago, we visited Nila Mack's children's storybook series "Let's Pretend." Its musical theme still resonates in my mind:

> "Cream of Wheat is so good to eat, yes we have
> it every day. We sing this song, it will make us
> strong, and it makes us shout 'Hurray! It's good
> for growing babies and grown-ups too to eat. For
> all the family's breakfast, you can't beat Cream of
> Wheat."

After the show I met the host, "Uncle Bill," at the bus stop; he gave me his autograph on his own copy of the script for the show ("To Hank, From 'Uncle' Bill Adams") - it's still somewhere in my garage today. In the Windy City, I also marched around the table with Don MacNeil at "The Breakfast Club" - little knowing that one of my best friends later in life eventually would be the boy singer on that morning show, Dick "Silver Throat" Noel.

In Hollywood, my parents took me to see "Smilin' Ed McConnell and his Buster Brown Gang." Smilin' Ed was a funky old man who sat at his Hammond organ playing loud and, I thought, very exciting music while his pet puppet Froggy plunked his magic twanger (you had to be there!). But I was mortified when one of the actors on the show thought my Mom's hat, which looked somewhat like a big-feathered brush, looked silly. He grabbed it right off her head, put it on, and ran around the studio while the audience cackled wildly. But all was forgiven by the ending of the program. I'll never forget how thrilled I was when Smilin' Ed cranked up the organ's volume to the threshold of pain and sang in his gravely voice,

> "The happy gang of Buster Brown now leaves the
> air - The happy gang of Buster Brown now leaves
> the air. So watch for us buddies next Saturday,
> We'll come with a bang and a BIG hurray, Buster
> Brown now leaves the air."

Believe it or not, I still have a tape of that show. Sometimes when I'm feeling low, I'll put it on. Within minutes, the world seems rosy again, and I'm up and at 'em - ready to conquer the world.

Like most kids, I played my own versions of "Let's Pretend" around the neighborhood. Playing cowboys and Indians, I made a stagecoach out of old orange crates and mounted it on an old "Flexible Flyer" wagon chassis. Somehow I got the other children to pull me around the block while I drove the coach (my version of Tom Sawyer whitewashing the fence, I guess). We put on shows in the back yard of our San Leandro home, dressing up in makeshift costumes from whatever apparel we could "borrow" from our parents. Ah, youth!

Music was an important part of my young life. I started piano lessons at the age of four, first from Hope Derry, then studying with Marion Radin and Gertrude Altman. When we would head out on Sunday drives around the San Francisco Bay Area, my Mom, Dad, and I would sing our heads off in three-part harmony as we drove down the highways and byways. It just came naturally to all of us. We would serenade ourselves and the traffic with,

> "We were sailing along on Moonlight Bay. You
> could hear the voices singing, they seemed to
> say."

I really think my love of music was almost genetic. One of my Dad's fondest memories was when his father surprised my grandmother in 1910 with a gift of a Victrola for the Jones family home. In their younger days, my folks relished the memory of seeing one of the first productions of "The Desert Song" and laughing when the leading man seemed to have more lipstick on than the ingénue. They had seen the renowned John Charles Thomas sing "The Lord's Prayer" at the 1939 World's Fair in San Francisco, accompanied by the man himself who had set it to music, Albert Hay Malotte. They told me when they had seen George M. Cohan himself dance and sing to his own "Yankee Doodle Dandy" at the same Fair and recalled how he berated the band for playing too slowly.

My Mom was an accomplished pianist and would practice and play often. I remember one time when I was about three or four she was at the piano and hit an absolutely beautiful chord. Somehow it moved me so much - just the sound of that one chord - that I ran to her and hugged her, begging her to play those same notes again and again. My Mom really didn't know what I meant or what I was feeling but tried to recapture that wonderful sound that had touched me. She couldn't find it again. I guess I was living a child's version of Arthur Sullivan's old classic song "The Lost Chord," the lyric of which ended:

"It may be only in heaven - I shall hear that grand Amen."

Whatever - music mattered greatly to me - right from the start.

My parents used to help run the San Leandro Town Meetings. It was a great concept in that world-renowned personalities and speakers came to our little town near Oakland to share their wisdom and experiences with an eager audience. My folks often would entertain the evening's speaker at our home for dinner prior to their presentation at the meeting. I well remember one night when I was about eight or nine years old. The speaker that evening came to our home for one of my Mom's fabulous chicken-in-sherry-wine dinners prior to her talk. Our guest was a rather short lady, sort of heavy-set, with short-cropped hair. The reason I remember her so well is that she seemed more interested in me than in my parents and their friends. She asked me what book I was reading, and I replied "*Treasure Island*." "Oh, I love that book too," she told me. Then she spotted the piano across the room and asked me if I played. I said, "I'm just learning." "Well, go ahead and play me a song," the nice woman requested. So I did (I think it was "Only Make Believe," from "*Showboat*"). "That's great," said my new friend. Then she invited me to sit on her lap and tell me more about my nine-year-old life. All I remember about that time on her lap is that she smelled *really* good.

About ten years ago, just before my Dad died, I was reminiscing with my parents about some of the fun-times we had together. I recalled that kind woman's visit to our home fondly and asked my folks, "Who was that nice lady that came to dinner - the one who I played the piano for and sat on her lap?" My Dad replied, "Oh that was Gertrude Stein. We liked her too!"

I guess that's where I first learned that, to paraphrase our distinguished guest, "A lap ... is a lap ... is a lap." (And no - she didn't offer me any brownies).

One of my earliest and best friends growing up was a kid who lived just around the corner from our San Leandro home, Dean Thompson. Our parents had been lifelong friends too: Al and Muriel Thompson and my parents were all members of "The Gang," a couples' group initially begun from younger members of the San Leandro First Methodist Church in the 1930s. Amazingly, their monthly "Gang Feed" lasted some sixty years, well into the 1990s. Dean was even in the same bassinet with me (I always used to say that I've never forgiven him for turning over in his sleep and squashing me against the rail). Who'd-a-thunk then that we'd both be pretty-much responsible for where the other one of us ended up in life some sixty-plus years later?

Everyone liked Dean. He just seemed to get along with everybody and had friends hanging from the rafters. He got his musical education early too, studying piano with a lively good local teacher named Mrs. Greer. Dean got to play more popular songs in his lessons than I did in mine which were more classically oriented. His Dad Al Thompson had a superlative tenor voice, much like the wonderful Swedish tenor Jussi Björling, so Dean was raised in a home with music all around too.

In 1950, our folks allowed Dean and me to go to San Francisco to see Dean Martin and Jerry Lewis in person at one of the city's big movie palaces. In between the showing of one of their early flicks, Martin and Lewis also did a radio broadcast from the stage of the theater that guest-starred their movie leading lady, French va-va-voom Corinne Calvet. We were absolutely enthralled with the madcap antics of Dean and Jerry - they almost bounced off the walls with energy as they did their act. It really was sensational. After the show, we went outside and watched them as they waved to the crowd below on the street and did shtick from their third floor theater dressing-room window. Man - this was show business!

We came home glowing from the experience. I'm afraid I was the initial hambone of the two of us. I basically did a "Mickey Rooney=Judy Garland" and said, "Hey Dean, let's put on a show!" We scribbled down what we could remember of the Martin and Lewis act and started mimicking what we saw -and who better on which to try out our routine than our parents' Gang Feed the following night. I was Jerry and Dean was Dean - or was it vice versa, I don't remember. We acted crazy, ran around a lot, and closed singing "Way Marie" as M&L did. I'm sure our captive audience didn't know quite what to make of us ten-year-old weirdos, but they laughed and applauded anyway. That lit the flame ... as the guy who cleaned up after the elephants in the circus replied when they asked him why he did what he did, "*what* - and give up show business??"

And so it began. We built platform stages in the rumpus room of my house and started putting on shows. We "broadcast" our plays and routines over "Station HJDT" (Hank Jones=Dean Thompson) and tried to fool the more gullible kids that we were really on the air (a few actually believed us). We put out a mimeographed newspaper to herald our attractions called "The Fun Time Gazette;" Dean was a really good artist and made the rag actually look pretty good. And we weren't beyond a little larceny either: we made joke phone-calls to random numbers pretending to be radio quiz programs (complete with musical backgrounds and phony applause); when "contestant" got the correct answer, they were promised a case of Oxodol soap (our supposed sponsor). This all blew up one day, however, when we mistakenly telephoned a random number we had previously called before, and the lady yelled back at us, "Where's the case of soap you promised me?" Oops!

In 1954, my parents gave me a Webcor tape recorder for Christmas. It was a heavy thing and technically primitive, but to me an absolute wonder. I wrote a script adapting Robert Louis Stevenson's pirate classic, "*Treasure Island.*" I then prodded my neighborhood friends to dramatize it and record it on the Webcor, complete with music and special sound effects. Long-time pals like Bill Faulkner and ever-patient Dean (who played Long John Silver's parrot yelping, "Pieces of eight, Pieces of eight") were drafted into participating in these mini-epics. I took the tape to Bancroft Junior High School and played it in English class to the befuddled amusement of my classmates who couldn't quite figure out what exactly was making my boat float.

My parents owned an old Bell & Howell 16mm camera, so I guess home-movies of these scripts were the next logical step. My cousin Harrison Bedell had introduced me to the world of 16mm early on with his creative and extremely imaginative use of his own camera. He did things with title cards, slow motion, reverse action, and other effects that still hold up today when I look at them. I stole much from Harrison's remarkable efforts when we made our first movie in 1954 when I was fourteen. It was called "Pirates Gold," a poor-man's version of *"Treasure Island,"* filmed at our home in San Leandro. Our house doubled as a colonial inn, and miniatures of the pirate ship were filmed in my Dad's backyard wheelbarrow with blue foodcoloring tinting the water to hopefully give the illusion of the stormy sea. Dean, Bill Faulkner, Russ Worley, and several of my other pals were strong-armed into appearing in the movie, bribed by free lunches of Danish æbelskiver pancakes cooked by my ever-patient and long-suffering mother. We projected the movie in a film process we invented called "Jonesoscope:" we put up old sheets on the rumpus room wall, took the projector outside on the patio some hundred feet away, and then filled up the screen (the sheets) with a picture almost life-size in its look (ah, technology!). I told you I was weird.

Further epics followed. We did our version of the Hardy Boys dime-novel *"Secret of the Old Mill,"* with Dean playing Frank Hardy and me as his brother Joe. We talked Southern Pacific Railroad into allowing us to use the engine of the wonderful old California Zephyr at the Oakland railroad yards, and the engineer even allowed us up into the cab to shoot. My poor Mom drove us all over the Bay Area for location shots, including out to Alamo where we filmed the climatic scene high up on the water tower of my Dad's walnut ranch there. Dean and Bill built a balsa-wood collapsible chair that was supposed to crumble when we hit one of the bad-guys over the head. Put it this way: his head crumbled more than the chair - but it looked good (and, to quote Fernando Lamas via Billy Crystal, "looking good is everything.")

The last movie we made was our version of the Dicken's classic, "*A Christmas Carol.*" Bob Conrad played Scrooge with a putty nose from my Max Factor "So-You-Wanna'-Be-An-Actor Kit." Dick McLain was a put-upon Bob Cratchit, and John "Pickle" Ravekes portrayed a German student on the streets of London. As it was a silent film, we never did figure out how the audience would know he was German, so John added a kind of Hitler gleam in his eye to fill in the blanks. We ran out of (my parents') money, so the world never saw this potential rival to "Citizen Kane," sorry to say. Oh well, there are always film festivals for revivals.

About this time (1954), I entered San Leandro High School. Under the guidance of two wonderful drama teachers - Sam Levine and Ken Soares, later to become dear friends and valued mentors - I appeared in every play and school musical presented there during my four-year tenure: "Our Town" (I played a dead kid in a graveyard); "Finian's Rainbow" (I was a black sharecropper - type casting); "The Night of January 16th" (I was a Prosecuting Attorney making pleas to Dean, who portrayed the Judge and who kept forgetting whether the script said he should say "overruled" or "sustained"); "Annie Get Your Gun" (the juvenile lead whose zaftig leading lady weighed almost twice as much as me); and "Beggar On Horseback" among many others.

But my shining hour at SLHS was playing the lead in Cole Porter's musical "Kiss Me Kate." Unfortunately, it required me to wear tights in the Shakespearian scenes; also unfortunately, my legs looked like they were stolen from the local chicken. To remedy this situation, Mr. Levine had a brainstorm idea of putting me in *four* pairs of tights to fill out my lower extremities; it was sort of the early San Leandro Hulk Hogan look. {Years later, I was doing a TV show with John Raitt, Bonnie's father, who had toured around the country playing the same character in "Kiss Me Kate" as I had. Trying to make conversation, I mentioned that I too had played the same lead part in school. Raitt looked me up and down evaluating my still-skinny frame and said, as if he didn't believe what he was hearing, "You DID??? Oh my, that's rather a *challenging* role, isn't it?"}

Then Elvis entered my life. From the first few bars of "Heartbreak Hotel" and on to "Ready Teddy," "Don't Be Cruel," and "All Shook Up," the Pied Piper of Tupelo spoke to me. His contagious rhythm, magnetic voice, and yes - his sense of danger, even in his music - became a siren call to this slightly pimply, super-skinny, downright nerdy devotee. Simply put, he got to me. The excitement we all felt when listening to an early Elvis record was the same thrill that so many of my age group experienced when we first heard Bill Haley's "Rock Around The Clock" a few years earlier or saw James Dean in "Rebel Without A Cause." They grabbed us - and seemed to speak for our generation. What else could I do then but form a rock-group to emulate "The King?" And so, in 1956, "Hank Jones and the White Bucks" was launched.

Poor Dean - he didn't have a prayer of having a quiet high school existence when I was around. He played absolutely terrific rock 'n roll piano and could out-Jerry Lee Lewis with his manic, pounding style. So he became the cornerstone of the "White Bucks" sound. Johnny Brumfield was the only student at San Leandro High who had an electric guitar, so he was drafted to join too - along with Gary Roderick on sax and Bill Johnson on drums. We went through the Elvis musical catalogue song by song, stealing licks and copying notes as we went along. As the singer, I tried to emulate the Presley style as skinny me, looking ridiculous, jiggled around the stage shaking my legs. I must confess I was awfully "white bread" (and I sure smiled too much when I sang). BUT, we were the first on campus to try something like this, and our response was good. It was almost like the kids were just waiting for us.

We were sort of an early "Garage Band" in that we woodshedded our arrangements in the lower den at Dean's house. The White Bucks first bookings were at military bases in the Bay Area and around Northern California. At one early engagement at the Alameda Naval Air Station (at the end of which Bill, our drummer, was so carried away he threw his drumsticks into the applauding crowd), a nicely-dressed middle-aged lady in the audience sent over her business card, offering help and encouragement. When I saw her name on the card ("Mary Rose Pool"), it didn't mean anything to me until she quietly explained she was Bing Crosby's sister. That got our attention. A Fan Club was formed. We recorded our first demos at Dick Vance Studios in Oakland in 1956 (my God, I've been recording for *50* years!) and later with Jack Hawkins at Sound Recorders and Richard Walberg in the living room of his house, both in San Francisco. A kind woman named Louise Ziviello asked to promote us and began sending gigs and contacts our way. Every Sunday afternoon we warmed up the crowd at San Leandro's Haycock's Steak House (but we still had to pay for our own meals there). We then proceeded to rock the house at high school assemblies throughout San Francisco and the East Bay, with occasional protests from the more uptight and conservative faculty members and quizzical stares from the kids at Oakland's predominantly black high schools ("what's up with these white boys?").

It was getting to be fun. The White Bucks won a big talent contest that disc jockey Charlie Stern put on at the Oakland Paramount Theater. The USO flew us to Arizona to entertain at the army bases there. To get there we wore parachutes on a non-pressurized DC3 troop transport - ouch, our poor ears never seemed to completely recover. That's where our sax man Gary Roderick met his future wife: Sherilyn was a chorus girl in "Alma's Dancing Darlings" (yes, *that* was their name) who toured with us. We performed regularly up at Rio Nido Resort on the Russian River and even had a small group of "groupies" who followed us from date to date (ah, the side-benefits of show-biz). Irv Glickman invited us to perform on Sundays at his prestigious "Jazz Showcase" in San Francisco. We didn't draw much of a crowd, but today it's still a kick to see our name on old posters advertising "Hank Jones & The White Bucks - COMING SOON: Dizzy Gillespie, Joe Williams, and Errol Garner" (all three of whom Dean and I would eventually work with a few years later). Dean and I used to drive to San Francisco at 5AM when we were in high school to be able to sit in the KSFO radio booth at the Fairmount Hotel with San Francisco's legendary DJ Don Sherwood and enjoy his mercurial talent; so it was a thrill when we won the call-in vote on his television talent show on KGO in 1957, rockin' the joint with "Let's Have A Party!" Our lack of taste came to the fore when we performed at Santa Rita Prison Farm and appallingly chose to close the show with "Jailhouse Rock!" (They obviously couldn't get Johnny Cash). Believe it or not, Mikey, they liked it!

As the popular TV series later reflected, they were indeed "Happy Days" back then in the 50s. "Hank Jones & The White Bucks" had become semi-big-fish in a small Bay Area pond. But in 1958, college beckoned, and the group had to be disbanded. It was off to San Jose State for Dean, and Stanford for me. But music and performing were now an important part of our lives, so Dean and I continued on singing as a duo. We had a good blend, Dean sang tenor, and I was the baritone. Did we ever work hard to get a good sound. Maybe it wasn't too commercial, but we sure sounded pretty, and our act grew to be "up" and lively.

We continued writing music together also, along with our San Leandro High classmate Larry Ray Hayes. Larry had come to California in 1956 after growing up in Colorado. He was a warm-hearted, open, friendly guy who liked to write poems and lyrics, and we all became great pals. The three of us worked hard writing tunes, some terrible, and gradually some darn good. Larry liked being known as "Larry Ray," and, because it sounded better, Dean dropped "Thompson" as his last name professionally and used "Kay" instead (his middle name being "Kermit"). So the songwriting team of Kay-Ray-Jones kept plugging along, writing mostly for the singing team of "Hank & Dean."

I never really felt a part of the Stanford scene. My official major there was in communications, but I really majored in "Hank & Dean." I must have been the only Stanford undergraduate who subscribed to *Cashbox* and *Variety* and devoured every issue. Every spare minute I had was spent rehearsing with Dean whenever we could get a break from our studies. I must admit though that my communications courses really did lay a good foundation for what live television was going to be like down the pike. I did my senior project in "TV directing" with fellow-student Ted Koppel, who was a househusband at the time; he was very talented (and he sure had great hair, even then). Also at Stanford, I helped at the student radio station with remote broadcasts from some of the rock concerts nearby, interviewing wild man Jerry Lee Lewis, "The Godfather of Soul" James Brown, and r&b pioneer Hank Ballard backstage for KZSU.

Dean and I continued to learn wherever and whenever we could. We regularly attended rock 'n roll shows at San Jose Civic Auditorium, almost like we were going to class. It was a terrific opportunity to get performance pointers and see the greats in person. We loved Fats Domino and his driving band; Fats had the biggest diamond ring on his pinkie that I'd ever seen - it was amazing he could play without tripping over it. Good Lord, what a beat he put down with that New Orleans stompin' sound. We also marveled at probably the best rock performer we'd ever seen - in my mind today, *still* the best: Jackie Wilson. He moved like a cat, sounded like an angel, and played the crowd like it was a violin. He was just like his hit "Baby Work Out," - he worked out. In fact he worked so hard, later on he eventually had a stroke right on stage that unfortunately ended his career. You think Michael Jackson and Elvis were hot in their prime? You should have seen Jackie Wilson!

And I'll never forget our experience with Bobby Darin. What a magnetic performer - what a talent! One night, summoning up our courage, we went backstage at San Jose Auditorium with our demos and asked "Mr. Splish-Splash" to give them a listen. He didn't have time then, but said to call him at his room at the Fairmount Hotel in San Francisco the next day and he'd see what he could do. So at noon, I called, and a sleepy Bobby Darin answered with a phlegmy "Hello." Oh God," I thought, "I woke him up." But he was cool and said to come up to his room in about an hour. We did. He greeted us with his morning stubble in a tee-shirt and jockey shorts. The first thing I noticed was that on the top of his bureau in his room was a carton - not a box, but a *carton* - of condoms. "Wow," I thought to myself, "this really *is* show business!" Dean and I played him several of our tunes on acetates, and Darin sent us down to the emotional basement when he told us in no uncertain terms that he thought they were lousy. But then, do you know what he did? He went over some of our songs section by section and suggested ways that would make them better. What a nice thing to do. He may have been an arrogant s.o.b. sometime to others, but he sure was kind and helpful to us.

Time marched on. Dean and I played college dates and charity events and attracted the interest of several San Francisco-based personal managers like Rita Braunstein, Hal Morris (Tony Martin's brother), and Norton Wais. Local disc jockeys like Ted Randall, Buck Herring, Gary Owens, and Casey Kasem (who eventually was to become a dear friend) urged us on. Even though we weren't quite ready, we auditioned for

several popular clubs in the Bay Area like "The Purple Onion."
I'll never forget that try-out because the owner/talent booker
we auditioned for at the club, Barry Drew, was found dead the
next weekend. We played at the "Toys For Tots" benefit at the
Marine's Memorial Auditorium with blue's great Jimmy
Witherspoon, at Richardson Springs Resort at Lake Tahoe, and
the Minstrel Club in San Jose - *anywhere* we could get
exposure.

It continued on. We appeared on the TV talent show
hosted by Ben Alexander, formerly Sergeant Joe Smith on
"Dragnet," and won on that program too; his associate Lucille
Bliss, an early Bay Area TV personality and later the queen of
voice-overs for cartoons, became a big booster. Our affinity for
prisons continued, and we celebrated New Years Eve 1961 by
performing for 2700 convicts at San Quentin; it was a weird gig
in that the cons were more interested in ogling the chorus girls
on the bill than in listening to us. I wonder why?? Then, after
much debate, we joined the American Guild of Variety Artists,
the San Francisco membership of which appeared to consist
only of strippers, female impersonators, and Hank & Dean.
Things were looking up.

My roommate freshman year at Stanford was a quiet,
husky good guy named Dave Pilkington from Southern
California. Both Dean and I owe a great debt to Dave and his
mother Doris because they allowed us to stay with them at their
home in La Cañada over several summers during vacation from
school. Their kind hospitality enabled us to have a home base
from which to operate as we made the rounds of record
companies and publishers in Hollywood to sell ourselves as
songwriters and recording artists. And when we were back up
north immersed in our college studies, our friend and co-writer
Larry Ray continued our efforts and hit the pavement for us.
Larry's faith in our talent and his dedication (and damn hard
work) were very much a factor in our eventual success. I can't
stress that enough.

Man, did we hustle! Beginning in 1959, I think we tried
to break down the doors at every record company and major
publisher in town. We hit on Snuff Garrett at Liberty, Lou Adler
at Dunhill, Mel Bly at Challenge, Lew Bedell at Dore, Jim
Harbert at Columbia, Lew Chudd and Eddie Ray at Imperial, Bud
Dant at Decca, and Dave Cavanaugh, Voyle Gilmore and Kent
Larson at Capitol, to name just a few. Our persistence paid off,

and we slowly got to be known to them - or at least to their secretaries. We had the best response from classy Tom Mack at Dot and dapper Eddie Shaw at Frank Sinatra's new Reprise label. One day Eddie, kind of a hood-like character straight out of Damon Runyon, told us he had to postpone our scheduled appointment because, as he whispered in a somewhat sinister tone that seemed dripping with hidden meaning, "*Frank's* in town!" It sounded awfully ominous, so we said that that was just fine with us and quickly headed for the door.

We tried hard to get agents and personal managers to sign us too, but it was tough. We had nibbles from Jimmy Rodger's manager Art Whiting, Morgan Montague, Alec & Helen Alexander, and John Vestal at the huge MCA Agency - all of whom liked us, but thought we needed more work. They were right. But in the fall of 1961, after spending our summer vacations persistently knocking on doors, flicking off rejection after rejection, and working very hard to improve our sound and material, things finally started to click. I kept a "Day At A Glance" Appointment Book close at hand to jot down the names of those we were seeing and how the meetings went, so it's fun to look back in those journals and see how it all came together. For example on August 30, 1961 I wrote:

> "Saw Steve Sholes at RCA. VERY NICE. Usually
> doesn't screen talent, but he promised to put in a
> favorable word to Neely Plumb. Maybe a
> break??!!"

For months, Dean and I had tried to see Neely Plumb, head of A&R at RCA Victor's Hollywood office. No luck. After barraging his secretary Pat Holbrook with phone calls and notes, we finally met the great man in the early part of the year. Neely liked our sound from the top, but thought the songs we wrote needed strengthening. (It didn't hurt that his young son Ben had just begun classes at Stanford, my alma mater, either). Further visits followed until we became familiar faces around the RCA offices, but still no talk of a deal. In late August, Dean and I drove all the way down from the Bay Area to see Neely for a scheduled meeting, but he was called away unexpectedly and couldn't make the appointment. We had driven four hundred miles for nothing. But Pat Holbrook, his girl Friday (and Saturday thru Thursday too), took pity on us and instead set up an interview with the national head of RCA A&R,

Steve Sholes, who just happened to be visiting LA that particular day from his Nashville home.

Steve Sholes was probably the most important creative producer on the label at the time. He biggest coup was engineering the deal with crafty Sam Phillips at Sun Records in Memphis that would bring Elvis Presley into the RCA fold. He did it, and this future member of the Country Music Hall of Fame would end up producing all the early classic Elvis sides on RCA like "Don't Be Cruel," "Teddy Bear," and "Hound Dog." He was a mountain of a man, just a huge physical presence, but with a gentleness about him and a soft voice that belied his massive size. Mr. S. listened to the musical demo of our sound and songs, smiled, nodded his head, and, as I noted in my journal, said he'd put in a good word for us with Neely (who worked *under* him). So in essence, by a fluke of a missed appointment, the boss at RCA had given us the nod of approval before his west coast producer had a chance to even present us to him as possible recording artists. The chain of command went out the window to our advantage.

The very next day we wrangled a long-sought-for audition at General Artists Corporation, one of the most important agencies in the entertainment business. As my trusty "Day At A Glance" book recorded:

> "August 31 1961: Met George Burke at GAC. We sang 'Sing Boy Sing,' 'Stormy Weather,' 'Dream Lover,' and (our own tune) 'Ain't Got A Nickel' for him. He kept saying over and over, "You boys are really good." He is *definitely* interested."

George Burke was a *wonderful* man. He had started in the show-biz trenches just barely out of his teenage years as a "gofer" on the old Milton Berle "Texaco Star Theater" Show. He used to love to regale us with Uncle Miltie stories, including how the madcap comic always wore a whistle around his neck and blew it loudly at everybody as he ordered them around the studio. Berle evidently wouldn't delegate authority to anybody and ran the show hands on - I mean *hands on.* George survived Berle and went on to his apprenticeship at GAC, eventually handling many of the important recording and nightclub acts the firm represented. And talk about timing: just as in the case of meeting Steve Sholes, the day we auditioned for George Burke at GAC was during the week he had decided finally to leave the agency, take a gamble, and form his own personal management firm with long-time friend and associate, Bill Weems; had we seen him two weeks earlier, it wouldn't have worked at all. As Dean and I basically were still green-behind-the-ears kids from small-town San Leandro, George was smart enough to drive up to the Bay Area with his lovely wife Gloria, meet our folks, and show that he was a family man and wasn't a stereotypical slick, fast-talking agent. George and Glo won us over in a second.

Whatta' week! The momentum continued. As my "Day At A Glance" Book noted:

"Sept 2 1961: Met Jimmy Haskell - Ricky Nelson's arranger, at his home. He liked our songs and style and offered help."

Jimmy Haskell was the talented man behind the popular Ricky Nelson sound that was sweeping America from coast to coast. He arranged and conducted the sessions for "Travelin' Man," "Hello Mary Lou," "Young Emotions," "A Teenage Romance," "I'm Walkin,'" and many other hit records by Ozzie's son (later he would arrange "Bridge Over Troubled Water," by Simon and Garfunkel, "Ode To Billy Jo," by Bobbie Gentry, "The Way You Look Tonight," by The Lettermen," and several of Elvis's biggest hits). In his apartment on Flores Avenue off of Sunset Blvd., we played him most everything we'd ever written and our current Hank & Dean demos. He listened closely, beamed, and promised to pass the word about us at Ricky's label, Imperial, as well as around town. And he did! And we promised Jimmy in return that, should we ever get on a label, he'd be our first choice to be our arranger on our sessions. And he was!

To provide the exciting capper to the month's good news, the next entry in my Day Book said it all:

"Oct 13 1961: Got a phone call from Neely Plumb offering us an RCA contract. We have flipped. That same night we auditioned at Bimbo's 365 Club (in San Francisco), and Bimbo said 'we were nothing short of terrific.'"

I'll never forget getting that call from Hollywood. I was back up north in San Leandro, the phone rang, and Pat Holbrook was on the line. She said, "Hank, Mr. Plumb is calling." I gulped, not knowing just what exactly he was going to say. Neely picked up the phone and said, "Hank, we want you and Dean to become part of the RCA family." All those years - yes, years of pounding the Hollywood pavement had paid off. All I could do was to stifle a big "wahoo." I couldn't wait to get hold of Dean at his San Jose State residence to tell him the good news. I called him there, but he was out. I alerted his housemother to have him call me in San Leandro immediately, but tried not to let on what was happening. When he finally called me back, Dean said, "What's up?" I said, "Nothing. Don't forget we've got that audition at Bimbo's 365 Club tonight, and oh, by the way, Neely Plumb just called us and offered us an RCA Victor recording contract." Dean practically dropped the telephone, and all I could hear on his end was shouting and screaming from my partner and his friends there. Honestly after all these years, I consider landing that deal with RCA *ourselves* - with no middle men, just us, a couple of college kids who worked our tails off to get on a major label - to be one of the proudest achievements of my life. The odds against that ever happening were formidable and nearly impossible. But son of a gun - WE DID IT!

Our producer Neely Plumb was quite a guy. He came from an old Georgia family and had been a saxophone player in several big bands. A real southern gentleman, he was soft-spoken with a dry sense of humor that made him easy to be around. His recording sessions were as laid back as the man himself. At RCA, he had some heavy-hitters in his stable of artists, including the then very popular "Limelighters" with Glenn Yarbrough, Esquivel, Ann Margaret, and Rod McKuen. Neely also produced the soundtracks for movies like "The Good, Bad, and the Ugly," "True Grit," and the hugely successful "The Sound of Music." Early on, I remember visiting him at his home and meeting his lovely family, including his wife, his daughter Flora, and youngest daughter Eve, then just a toddler; Eve eventually found fame portraying Jan Brady on the classic sit-com "The Brady Bunch."

I'll never forget the actual signing with RCA Victor at their Hollywood offices. As we literally were putting pen in hand to write our names on the contract, from down the hall there came probably the most haunting sound I'd ever heard. It was the sound of a lone harmonica playing an absolutely beautiful brand new song backed with full orchestra and a huge vocal group. The studio door was open as everyone was listening to the playback, and the melody wafted throughout the entire building. I choked up - it was SO pretty. I found out later that we were listening to Henry Mancini actually recording "Moon River" from "Breakfast at Tiffany's" at that very moment. Ever since then, whenever I hear that song, I remember that Dean and I were right there from its birth. It's a very special memory I'll never forget.

At first, a small faction of the administrative brass at RCA tried to make a provision of our contract that they would release our records on their new subsidiary Groove Records which they were trying to get off the ground. A few executives even thought of teaming us with a girl duo on that smaller label. When we heard that one of the songs they wanted us to record with the girls was called "Dum Dum," we instructed George Burke, already functioning as our manager, to tell them a big "NO!:" "we didn't break our butts all those years to end up singing "Dum Dum" with a girl group we didn't even know." Neely agreed, and the whole concept was dropped. But it gave us a heads up as to how corporate politics would and could sometimes try to influence creative decisions. Isn't it terrific that that's all a thing of the past? Yea, sure.

Having signed with RCA in October, the company wanted us to get out a Christmas release immediately before the holiday season. After going over quite a few Christmas songs with Neely, we settled on the best of the batch: a pretty ballad entitled "Christmas Village" and a Hawaiian number called (Oh God, here goes) "Deck The Hut With Coconut." (Hey, ya' gotta' start someplace). Then, I think to appease us, RCA also allowed us to record one of our own self-penned up-tempo songs, "I'm Gonna' Build Myself A Raft." So at 2 PM on Friday, October 27, 1961 in cavernous Studio One at the NBC/RCA Building at Sunset & Vine in Hollywood, we showed up - ready to sing. We kept our word to Jimmy Haskell and asked that he be hired to arrange the date. Jimmy worked right up to the deadline, and we saw him literally leaping over a hedge with sheet music in hand to make it to the studio at 1:59 PM.

Jimmy handpicked our musicians, most of whom initially were straight out of Ricky Nelson's group. Over several years recording on the RCA label, we had the cream of the crop backing us up on our singles and album. Bear with me as I name them, because I am *so* proud to have been associated at least for a time with these musical legends.

Were we ever blessed. On guitar we had LA's most popular session man, Tommy Tedesco and also the picker whom Bruce Springstein has called "the best rock 'n roll guitarist ever" - James Burton (James later went on to be lead guitar for Elvis on all his later hits like "Suspicious Minds" and "In The Ghetto" as well as his many concerts dates. Supposedly, when James heard that Elvis had died in Memphis in 1977, his first words were, "Does anybody know John Denver's home phone number?"). Other guitarists we also used were Allan Reuss on rhythm guitar and jazz great Barney Kessell on some of the more subtle numbers. Glen Campbell was to lend his distinctive 12-string guitar to our records later on.

Our piano men were Leon Russell (yes - *that* Leon Russell), and also Bob Florence, and Ernie Freeman. We worked with "The Fifth Beatle" on organ Billy Preston a few years later. On drums the beat was usually laid down by LA's top session man Hal Blaine (who got the groove going on "I Got You Babe," "California Dreamin'," "Be My Baby," "MacArthur Park," the Beach Boys "Pet Sounds," on and on); Earl Palmer, Hal's rival in town. subbed when Blaine was busy. Harmonica was blown by the great Toots Thielemans; it was Toots, I found out later, who gave Henry Mancini's "Moon River" such an unworldly beautiful sound. Carol Kaye, without doubt the best female bass player in America, graced every one of our RCA dates. Our string section was made up largely from members of the Los Angeles Philharmonic; they loved working with Jimmy Haskell, because he was known for his skill at string arrangements. As the capper, our sax man was Plas Johnson, the man who made the cartoon "The Pink Panther" come alive with those contagious, lilting riffs.

Vocally for the rock numbers, our background girl singers were Darlene Love and "The Blossoms;" Darlene, who had mega hits with Phil Spector like "He's A Rebel" and "Da Doo Run Run" when she was singing lead with "The Crystals," is still active some forty years later; she makes her regular appearance every December on "Late Night With David Letterman" singing her Spector Christmas hits and invariably tears the joint down. The big vocal group we worked with on some of the prettier ballads was captained by Jack Halloran whose singers included super-dooper bass man Thurl Ravenscroft (remembered for his booming low register on Rosie

Clooney's "This Ole House" and being "Tony The Tiger" on commercials) and ethereal soprano Loulie Jean Norman (whose flawless voice enhanced so many Sinatra and Mathis recordings, but is most noted for her wailing siren call on the "Star Trek" theme). Talk about "The A Team!" All these musicians and singers were put down on 4-track tape (yes – only <u>4</u> tracks) by our engineer, Al Schmitt, who today is considered to be almost the Godfather of modern recording engineering.

A record session in 1961 and 1962 was much different than those today. The formula usually was then that you put down four songs in three hours, with very little "tracking" done to clean up the mistakes. The orchestra was right there in the studio with the vocalist. Every musician and each singer was trying his darnedest not to screw up: nobody wanted to look bad in front of everybody else.

I used to run into Sinatra's arranger Nelson Riddle at Musso & Frank's Grill in Hollywood. He was one of the saddest looking souls I ever met, that is until you started talking music with him. Then he lit up. One day about 1980 when we both were eating lunch at the counter, I asked him if anyone still recorded that old, wonderful way, with the full orchestra there. He said wistfully, "No, not really - only in some of the Latin American countries and Japan. It was great then, wasn't it? I miss those days so much." Me too. There was a sense of danger in those sessions - adrenalin makes good music.

The RCA studio looked like an aircraft hanger, it was so big. The engineer's booth was separated from the musicians and us by a huge glass window. Ten-foot speakers were placed around the studio for playback. Never in my life will I forget the thrill of hearing Take #1 of "Christmas Village," the first song we ever recorded on RCA, played back at full volume over those speakers, complete with a full orchestra and chorus and our two voices soaring over the ensemble. Lumps in throat, shivers, goose-bumps, tears - all of the above in response to the emotion of hearing our dream come true. We'd worked so hard to get there, and finally here it was.

Unfortunately however, when played for the executives at the label, the two Christmas songs didn't cut the mustard. They felt that they weren't strong enough to merit a release before the holidays. As much as we liked hearing ourselves on a professional record with all the bells and whistles, honestly we didn't think so either. For our next session, it was back to our trunk of songs.

DEAN THOMPSON & HANK JONES REHEARSING SHOWS FOR THE
NEIGHBORHOOD KIDS IN SAN LEANDRO, 1951

GROWING UP & MAKING 16MM MOVIES WITH MY FRIENDS - 1955

(TOP LEFT) FILMING "A CHRISTMAS CAROL" WITH DICK MCLAIN & BOB CONRAD
(TOP RIGHT) FILMING "SECRET OF THE OLD MILL" WITH DEAN THOMPSON
(BOTTOM LEFT & RIGHT) WORKING ON FILM PROJECTS WITH DEAN

HANK JONES & THE WHITE BUCKS – 1957
(Left to right: Dean Kay Thompson – piano; Gary Roderick – sax;
Bill Johnson – drums; Hank Jones – vocal; John Brumfield – guitar)

HANK JONES & THE WHITE BUCKS ON TV - 1958

HANK JONES & THE WHITE BUCKS
WITH SAN FRANCISCO RADIO & TV PERSONALITY DON SHERWOOD

HANK JONES - 1958

DEAN KAY - 1958

AT THE FAIRMONT HOTEL IN SAN FRANCISCO READY TO HEAR TONY BENNETT
HANK JONES, MANAGER GEORGE BURKE, & DEAN KAY

HANK & DEAN RECORDING AT
RCA VICTOR STUDIOS, 1961

RCA VICTOR SESSION , OCTOBER 1961

(TOP) JIMMY HASKELL, H & D, NEELY PLUMB

(MIDDLE) NEELY PLUMB & HANK & DEAN

(BOTTOM) NEELY PLUMB & HANK & DEAN

A Sensational, New Singing Team Has Arrived With An Exciting, Swingin' Album!

ARRIVAL TIME

recorded by

HANK AND DEAN
JONES   KAY

Side 1
IVORY TOWER
LET IT HAPPEN AGAIN
BILLY BOY
THERE'S A LONG, LONG TRAIL
MEMORIES ARE MADE OF THIS
HARBOR LIGHTS

Side 2
LET THE REST OF THE WORLD GO BY
WISHIN' WELL
A LOVELY WAY TO SPEND AN EVENING
SENTIMENTAL JOURNEY
WHO'S IT GONNA BE?
SING BOY, SING

on RCA VICTOR • LPM/LSP–2570 • MONAURAL and STEREO

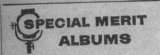

SPECIAL MERIT ALBUMS

— Pop Talent —

ARRIVAL TIME
Hank Jones and Dean Kay. RCA Victor LPM 2570 (M);
LSP 2570 (S)—Hank Jones and Dean Kay, who are featured on the Tennessee Ernie Ford Show, make a solid
debut on this, their first recording. The duo show off
their vocal ability with such tunes as "Ivory Tower,"
"There's a Long, Long Trail," "Let the Rest of the World
Go By" and "Sentimental Journey." Their blend is unusual
and their style is fresh and imaginative. Talented lads
should go far.

VARIETY   Wednesday, November 14, 1962

Top Singles Of The Week
(The 'Best Bets' of This Week's 100-Plus Releases)

HANK & DEAN . . . . OLD DEVIL MOON
(RCA Victor) . . . . And They Did
Hank Jones & Dean Kay's "Old Devil Moon" (Players Music*)
dishes up this great showtune with a modern beat and an arresting sound which should give it a potent spinning lift. "And
They Did" (Pampert) is another highly commercial side with
a good teenage lyric.

PICKIN' PEAS WITH TENNESSEE ERNIE

In early January 1962, a news release went out from ABC-TV in San Francisco. It noted that:

> "The hottest singing assignments in daytime television will be filled in San Francisco next month. Posts are open for one girl vocalist and two boy singers with the new 'Tennessee Ernie Ford Show.' Search for the three young singers opens on Saturday, January 6, when Tennessee Ernie and producer Bill Burch will screen applicants in KGO-TV's Studio A from 10 a.m. to 12 noon. Singing auditions will be scheduled at a later date. The two boy singers should be between the ages of 18 and 30, with some experience preferred. Ernie is putting out the call for the singers first in the Bay Area, hoping to discover new singing stars on his own home ground."

Dave Houser, a veteran newspaperman at the San Leandro Morning News, alerted us to the big search right away. Fortunately, Bill Weems, our co-manager with George Burke, knew the show's producer; he alerted Bill Burch to be sort of on the lookout for us amidst the throng of applicants. 1,100 vocalists showed up to audition, screened by Burch, Ford's manager Jim Loakes, and Dale Sheets of Music Corporation of America. From the original 1,100 who auditioned, the number was whittled down to 17, and then – Oh-Ma' God! - just down to "Hank and Dean." We got it! Dave Houser at the Morning News followed us on journey the entire way, with long articles that started with headlines that said, "Is That Opportunity Knocking For Local Singers?," ending up with "Local Boys Make Good," and finally "Hank and Dean A Hit!"

Ernie Ford held a press conference announcing our signing. Newspapers reported:

> "In a press conference yesterday, Ernie gave an indication of how highly he regards the potential of Hank and Dean. He pointed out that he told the two 22-year-olds that he didn't want

them to quit school or even miss a class (Hank is a senior at Stanford, Dean a senior at San Jose State). "Fine!" the youths chorused. "That's just the way we wanted to do it, if we could." "Well, whether you wanted to or not, that's the way it would have to be," declared Ol' Ern. "And don't worry about working your schedule in with ours. We'll work ours around you!"

We still had a long way to go to prepare for the pressure and responsibility of being featured on a 5-day-a-week national daytime television show. One thing Ernie wanted was to include us in the hymns he sang at the end of every program; his spiritual albums on Capitol Records were huge sellers, and closing each show with a hymn was his trademark on previous television outings. Dean and I had a pretty good backlog of songs we could do in our solo spots, but sure needed help in woodshedding the hymns and learning the intricate harmonies they contained.

That's when Dick Noel arrived on the scene. He had been hired as the "boy singer" on the show to take some of the vocal pressure off Ernie and croon the popular standards and classic love songs that he had sung so well over the years. He had been featured vocalist with the Ray Anthony Band and on radio with Don MacNeil's popular "Breakfast Club" program from Chicago. As a side effort, he also was asked to whip two green college kids into shape vocally and teach them the basics of sightreading music and group singing. Thanks to Dick's skill and patience (along with a large dollop of humor), we gradually got pretty darn good at blending in with the two older pros. With Dick's smooth baritone, Dean's high tenor, my second baritone, and then Ernie's rich, deep bass, the hymns (and later the Barbershop Quartet numbers) sounded GOOD, if I do say so myself.

The pre-buzz on the show was mixed to say the least. Bill Fiset in the Oakland Tribune said before the program aired that "those who've seen the tapings of the new 'Ernie Ford Show' done in San Francisco to start Monday say it's really bad. Two Oakland boys, Hank Jones and Dean Kay, will folk-sing on the show, and they're supposed to be the saving grace." Dave Houser of the Morning News countered his Oakland rival by saying that the Oakland paper seemed to be following the San

Francisco style of claiming everything in sight as its own, and that "Hank and Dean have lived in San Leandro all their lives and only went to Oakland to be born 22 years ago." Houser also added that the reaction he heard to the show that was just the opposite of what Fiset reported, and that "the daytime series is shaping up as strong as many evening variety shows. We'll let the viewers decide."

After weeks of rehearsal, the new ABC-TV Tennessee Ernie Ford Show made its debut across America and Canada on April 2, 1962. In truth, it was, like most shows finding their way, a work in progress. Early reviews loved Ernie (of course he opened singing his mega-hit "16 Tons") and the silky voice of Dick Noel, but almost unanimously panned the frequency of the commercials inflicted upon the viewers. Terrence O'Flaherty of the San Francisco Chronicle mentioned that Ford surrounded himself with a group of lively personalities, "including a pair who call themselves 'Hank and Dean.'" *Variety* said, that compared to Ford, "Hank Jones and Dean Kay, of some collegiate note who sang 'The Sloop John B.,'" were still not dry behind the ears in projecting a rhythm." The Hollywood Reporter noted that the other four vocalists on the program were Dick Noel, Anita Gordon, Hank Jones and Dean Kay, and that "all four warblers were capable." Dwight Newton in the San Francisco Examiner kindly noted that "the liveliest bit was contributed by Hank Jones (Stanford) and Dean Kay (San Jose State), Oakland-born boys who have been friends since childhood. Very good. They almost made you forgive the constipation commercial!"

We worked hard to get better. Jim Flood, an ABC publicist, in a newspaper interview said, "When I happened to hear Hank and Dean audition, I thought they were pretty good. Then I heard them again the other day and - WOW - have they improved." We sure tried. Our featured spot on each show ran the gamut of musical styles and genres, from folk to pop to rock to country and western. After a few weeks on the air, Ernie told us how much his parents back in Bristol, Tennessee liked us: that helped! And on our 260th show, he added a warm "p.s." to a note producer/director Bill Burch wrote, thanking us for our participation in making the program a winner. That *really* made us feel good. We sort of knew we "arrived" when Dean and I were used as a question one week in the *TV Guide* crossword puzzle: "Hank & Dean, 36 across, 4 letters:" (Answer) "Duet."

With Ernest Jennings Ford, what you saw - was what you got! He was a down-home, fun-loving, *very* talented, good guy, somehow thrust into the limelight with no place to hide. It was easy to be caught up in the excitement around him, but it was kind of sad to see. When you ate with him in a restaurant, Ernie often would have to sit in the back booth, facing the wall. Otherwise, his meals would be a series of constant interruptions by well-meaning strangers eager to get his autograph and socialize with him. And you almost took your life in your hands when you drove in a car with him. People would pull alongside, recognize him, and in their excitement, start to swerve into his lane of traffic. All privacy went out the window with his success. But Ernie was always was so patient with his fans, and pretty much accepted the whole thing as "part of the territory."

But oh, he had a wild side. One day we started the taping of a show in the afternoon after Ern had had a couple martinis for lunch. We filmed his opening number right on the street on Golden Gate Avenue in San Francisco in front of the ABC-TV Studios. There was Ford in the middle of all the traffic and pedestrians singing, "San Francisco - open your Golden Gate" as Jeanette MacDonald had done in the movie. At the end of his big finish of the song, Ernie, quite unplanned, promptly hailed a cab, got in, and headed for home to the utter dismay of the director and everybody in the control booth. All you could hear over the headsets was, "Where is he?!" Where did he go?!" What are we going to do?"

Then there was the time Ford decided he'd give me lessons on the air on how to milk a real cow. Unbeknownst to yours truly, he called me over to my new friend and proceeded to teach me what to do and where to pull (I muttered something about "being *utterly* confused and not having the *hang* of it"). But then when I succeeded in obtaining only a few dribbles from Bossy, Ernie promptly took over. He grabbed a tit, and started squirting streams of fresh milk directly from the cow on to Dick Noel and every crewmember around the studio in the line of fire, cackling and laughing uproariously all the way. You just never knew what he would do next.

Ernie Ford's "Sixteen Tons" remains the fastest selling record in Capitol Records history. But it was his hymn albums that were the biggest and most consistent sellers over the years. Dean and I were honored to appear with him on his *I Love To Tell The Story* album and backed Ernie up on his moving rendition of "How Great Thou Art." (RCA allowed us to do this on their competitor's label with a liner note that said, "Hank Jones & Dean Kay appear through the courtesy of RCA Victor Records").

Ernie's true nature and sincerity really came through on those old classic spirituals. Believe it or not, we recorded the entire twelve songs on the *I Love To Tell The Story* album in one day, usually with only one or two takes per song. It was a testament to Ford's talent, skill, and savvy that we were able to do this. Our version of "How Great Thou Art" with Ernie is still in release today on compilation CDs and sounds as good now as it did then. That's special to me, as it was my parents' favorite hymn.

I guess my ultimate claim to fame in the blooper department took place in 1963 during one of the closing hymns. As I said, the hymn was sort of Ernie's trademark - he had that wonderfully rich, bass voice and great sincerity that would send the chills down your spine whenever he sang. Although we had loads of fun and could cut-up on other segments of the program, it was an unspoken rule that we *never* kidded around during the hymn.

One particular day just prior to the closing, Dean and I sang a musical number from our then-current RCA album. We were dressed in casual outfits for that song, but then had to dash backstage for a quick change into the suits we were to wear for the hymn. Unfortunately, in the rush, I neglected to zip one very crucial part of my apparel.

Thinking that all was well, I ran onstage unawares and stood next to Ernie, ready to sing. We looked especially distinguished and dignified in our dark suits that day, standing with our hands folded in front of us against an illuminated cross as our backdrop. Immediately, the floor-manager began to count down, "5, 4, 3 ...." At that precise moment, Ernie happened to glance over at me. He looked down, did a double-take, and whispered urgently out of the corner of his mouth ...

"DON'T WAVE BYE-BYE!"

But it was too late - we were back on the air, singing our little hearts out. I don't know how we got through "Peace in The Valley" without "losing it," but somehow we did. The panic of that moment has sort of made everything a blur, but I do remember one thing: I kept my trembling hands clasped tightly in front of me, and when it came time to wave bye-bye ...

it was the *quickest* wave you've ever seen!

The Ford Show was such a happy experience. The crew became family to the cast too. One of the guys behind the scenes was a funny man named Don Gold, known affectionately to one and all as "SJ." "SJ" stood for "Super Jew," as Don felt his ethnic group also needed representation among all us hymn-singing Christians. He loved to play pranks on us. One day at dress rehearsal, Ernie was singing "Were You There When They Crucified My Lord?" From behind the curtain in back of us came Don's voice yelling, "Yes I 'vas!" Sometimes at rehearsal when we were singing a sacred song in front of a beautifully illuminated cross, the cross mysteriously would be raised and the Star of David lowered in its place for equal time, all thanks to our beloved "SJ."

Ernie, Dean, Dick Noel, Anita Gordon, Jim Lange, and I would usually eat lunch together at Oreste's, one of San Francisco's finest Italian restaurants. Fresh dungeness crab, veal scaloppini, linguini with clams - I still can taste their specialties. It was such a kick to see all the double-takes people would give "the Old Peapicker" when he nonchalantly strolled in for a meal. Other times, if we were on a shorter break, we went to diners and fast-food establishment near the ABC Studios. On one hurried lunch expedition, we stopped at the stoplight before crossing the street and noticed a disheveled old lady next to us holding her dog. She put the dog down on the pavement in order to push the button to change the light to green. Only then did we realize that not only was the dog dead, but it was stuffed. Trying not to "lose it," we headed for the local greasy-spoon where the Asian waitress in the most broken English imaginable inquired what kind of dressing we wanted on our salad. She told us they were offering "french," "<u>t</u>ousand island," or "roak-a-fuck." We invariably chose the latter variety, just so she would repeat it again for us.

Then there was "the screw." It was an inconsequential metal appendage to a post separating the Ford Show set from the audience in the ABC-TV studio. Nobody really remembers why or how it all started, but one day Dick Noel decided to unscrew "the screw" and give it to our associate producer, Bill Martin. He simply said, "Here Bill, take this." Bill, one of the nicest fellows on the planet, didn't know quite what to make of his new gift and said, "I don't want this." Whereupon Noel just walked away leaving the little do-dad in Bill's open hand. A few weeks later Bill Martin figured out a way to surreptitiously slip the screw back into Dick's hand at a moment he wasn't expecting it. And so "The Great Screw Duel" began - passed back and forth at inopportune moments from Dick Noel to Bill Martin and back again. This running gag has lasted some forty-plus years and still goes on to this day.

Some of the "passings of the screw" are classics. On Dick's birthday celebrated on the air, Bill arranged to have the screw baked inside the fancy birthday cake that Dick then found on his first bite. When Bill had a serious operation in the hospital, Dick arranged through Bill's wife Lola to have the doctor show Bill what was causing the blockage in his system that had been removed during surgery: you guessed it - the screw! When Dick went skiing up in the mountains, he found the screw mysteriously appearing in a cabin closet at the bottom of one of his ski boots. Then Lola Martin gave Bill "the screw" - with greetings from Dick - during a romantic moment in their connubial bed. On and on ...

Some "Tennessee Ernie Ford Shows" still stand out in my mind. One day we had a guest on during one of the talk segments who supposedly was the mother of a famous television personality. Ernie, Dick, Anita Gordon, Dean and I all had to figure out who she was. The segment was milked for a good six or seven minutes until someone finally guessed that the woman was *my* mother {Dean and I played dumb, which wasn't that hard to do). My Mom was a great sport about being in on the gag. On another show, Dean, Dick, Jim Lange (our announcer), and I had to diaper a live pig. That future piece of bacon squirted everywhere, especially on me and the dark suit I was planning to wear on the next hymn segment. We learned one of life's great lessons on that show: "pig pee smells!" On yet another program, Dean and I were to sing the old standard "Way Back Home" on a backyard barbeque set. We had rehearsed the song with no problem earlier, but on the air for the first time the crew actually lit the fire so it would look more real. That damn barbeque bellowed so much smoke that we ended up coughing and hacking our way through the whole number, much to the delight of Ernie laughing uproariously off camera.

Dean and I almost closed the show down one day. We were to sing a duet on two stools with a floor microphone in between us to pick up our voices. As Ike Hunter, our floor manager, was counting down the seconds we had left before we went on the air "10-9-8-7 ...," I realized at about "6" that the mike was pointed directly at me and not in between us as it should be which would ensure that the sound engineer was picking up a good blend of both our voices. So, since there was absolutely no time to call a technician to change the mike, I just tweaked it a bit so it pointed midway between us. You would have thought I'd murdered a baby. The union crew called a "grievance" and said we were taking away their work by not calling a stagehand to do the job. It didn't make any difference that there was no time to do it and, if I hadn't moved the mike, we would have sounded terrible. Ah, lessons learned. From then on, I didn't touch one technical thing.

We sometimes would tape the shows away from the ABC studio just to give them some variety. For instance, we filmed five programs at Bill Harrah's Casino at Lake Tahoe (Dean and I stayed in the same hotel room there from which Frank Sinatra Jr. would be kidnapped some months later). I looked much younger than my 22 years in those days, so Ernie and Dick Noel decided to have a little fun: they went to every security guard on the Harrah's premises and told them I was underage. So wherever I went for that entire week on casino property, I was carded and had to stop and show my ID to the staff. The rats!

As the weeks rolled on and more shows were broadcast, fan mail started to come in. At first, we employed "Hollywood Fan Mail Service" to answer all the letters, but they proved to be too impersonal in their responses (and too expensive too). A good solution was reached when we hired Linda De Maria, wife of our song-writing partner Larry Ray, to handle the mail. Linda was great at sorting it all out, sending pictures, and giving each response a nice personal touch.

Some viewers would write us every week, like Donna Jean Imboden, a country girl from Minersville, Ohio. She closed each letter with "KSYLSMBTW," which we finally figured out was "Keep smiling - you look so much better that way." Donna Jean's devotion to Hank & Dean kind got a little out of hand, as she eventually named her firstborn set of twins "Hank & Deana" (I kid you not!). Mrs. Ethel M. Brown of Detroit also wrote regularly. She was a slightly deaf widow lady who kept asking us to sing "Vaya Con Dios" whenever we could. Every so often after the closing hymn when we all were waving "bye-bye" while the credits rolled over our faces, I would try to silently mouth "Goodbye, Mrs. Brown" to her. She liked that. And once in a while we would receive notes from fellow performers that made us smile. The kinetic Bobby Lewis, who had the classic rock and roll hit "Tossin' and Turnin," wrote to say how much he enjoyed seeing us on TV every day, that we all were in the performing brotherhood, and to keep "spreadin' the joy." He's always signed his letters "Bobby T. T. Lewis."

Susan Engel of Fraser, Michigan, a young high school girl, was another loyal fan. We kept up a correspondence for years that eventually developed into a deep friendship. Sue always wanted to go into show business and came to California to pursue her dream, staying with Lori and me in North Hollywood for several months when she worked at Universal Studios. As "Sue Mathis," she eventually went into broadcasting and developed a reputation as a fine national news reporter on television. She then left broadcasting and worked her way up to a high position in the Reagan White House, including a stint as an aide to Jim Brady before he was shot. Sue married a wonderful guy named Bob Richard and had a daughter, Meredith (now a very talented budding actress/singer with an eye toward a career in theater). We kept in close contact and had mutual visits before Sue's untimely death a few years ago. As Sue proved so well, a fan can end up being a dear friend too.

You never knew what would turn up in the fan mail. One day on the show I mentioned that I had been to most of the 50 states, but had never been to Montana. In next week's mail was a letter from a Mrs. Francy Shaver inviting Dean and me to spend the holidays with her family in Deer Lodge, Montana: "Your time is our time! Our house is your house!" Patricia Hoffman in the mid-west wrote that "Every time Hank appears on the screen my daughter Julie simply squeals with delight and makes remarks like 'I'd like to have him to play with ...' This goes on and on. By the way, Julie is 4 old." On one occasion, a little girl about the same age was standing in line to get into the studio with her mother. The ABC page came backstage and said the lady said her child was the BIGGEST "Hank & Dean" fan, never missed us on TV, and would love to meet us. So we went outside to where she was just to say "hello." The moment that child took a look at us in person she burst into tears and ran down the street with her mother chasing her the whole block. I still have that effect on women, no matter what their age.

One of the great benefits of being on a 5-day-a-week national television show was that it gave us the opportunity to work with and get to know some outstanding talent who would show up as guest artists on the program. What a treat and what a thrill! For example, country music legend Patsy Cline was on the Ford Show with us. She was an earthy, warm, down-home woman who was a real hoot. When she did our show, she had been recovering from a terrible auto accident that had left her black and blue and even had scraped off some of her scalp. To cover that up, she wore a humongous black wig to hide the scars. She delighted in pulling her wig back and showing us all the damage that had been done and what remained to heal. How ironic then that just a few weeks after appearing on our show and knocking us all dead with her poignant country ballads, Patsy would die in a fiery plane crash on her way to perform to an audience of devoted fans. What a loss. Sweet Dreams, Patsy.

Bob Hope came on to plug one of his many books. He was slick - was he ever "Mr. Cool." Dapper and oh-so-smooth, he *knew* he was Bob Hope! His timing was like a Swiss watch, and he played an audience better than anyone I've ever seen. And Lord did he *need* those laughs and applause: they were like mother's milk to him. I've never seen anything like it. Some ten years later, we ended up living within a half a mile of each other in Toluca Lake. I'd see Mr. H. driving around a lot, usually at about 7 PM, heading for the local Baskin Robins for his nightly ice cream cone. I knew several Hope staff members and writers who accompanied him over the years on his USO Tours, and they told me it wasn't just ice cream that he was headed for those many nights: supposedly he had assorted chorus girls and pretty starlets stashed in apartments throughout Toluca Lake to enjoy the cones with him. Whatta' guy!

Jimmy Dean came in for a whole week to spell Ernie when he went on vacation. What a piece of work he was. I'm afraid the cast decided that, hands down, "Mr. Big Bad John" was probably the dirtiest and most repulsive man we'd ever met. Jimmy's specialty was telling us the foulest, most off-color joke he could think of just before we had to sing the *hymn* at the end of the show. He then would immediately change to his pious look when the cameras rolled, and it was time to sing with great sincerity about "Precious Jesus." Jimmy Dean also enjoyed startling any and all individuals conversing with him by, out of the blue, unzipping his fly and letting it all hang out, so to speak, until someone noticed. I'm not kidding. No wonder he ended up in the sausage business.

Jimmy Dean's crassness was counterbalanced by Minnie Pearl's goodness. Talk about a sweetheart - Minnie was one of the kindest, nicest and most giving people I've ever met. Even though she hid behind her countrified image as Cousin Minnie from Grinder's Switch, in reality she was a leader of Nashville society, Sarah Ophelia Colley - Mrs. Henry Cannon. Minnie appeared many times on the Ford Show, even traveling to the flight deck of the USS HANCOCK with us to broadcast the program as we entertained hundreds of navy men and women in uniform. She and Ernie had almost a country-comic-shorthand going on between them: they could break each other up over and over again by just starting to tell a few words of a familiar story or joke they'd each heard a million times before. On one show, I played Minnie's younger boyfriend singing "Does Your Mother Know Your Out - Cecilia?" as I tried to woo her to sit with me on the couch and fool around. I must say that we really played well off each other, and that sketch got lots of laughs. It's funny now some forty years later how one recalls little things, but I remember that in our quasi-romantic comical clinches performing that number Minnie smelled *so* good. She wore no perfume at all - just old fashioned, pure, sweet-scented soap - as pure and as sweet as she really was. Afterwards, Minnie took me aside and quietly told me that I had the best natural comic talent she'd run into since she teamed with Rod Brasfield, her late partner on "Grand Ole' Opry." I couldn't believe that that was true, but I was puffed up for weeks after her generous compliment.

Cliff Arquette was another frequent visitor to the show: you may remember him better as "Charley Weaver." Cliff was a super-bright guy, whose randy wit could top any seasoned comic. He later used it to great success during his years as a regular on TV's "Hollywood Squares." You never knew what he was going to pull: one time Dean and I were lip-synching our RCA single of "Ain't Got A Nickel" in a soda-shop set, and we looked up to see Cliff as Charley Weaver unexpectedly looking longingly at our chocolate sundaes through the window of the store. How we ever got through that song without breaking up I'll never know. And oh did Cliff love the ladies! He had an ongoing campaign to get to first base with our wardrobe lady,

Hazel Dewey. I don't know if he ever did, but I do know Hazel sure enjoyed the chase. But there was another side to Cliff Arquette too: he was a genuine civil war buff and scholar and even opened his own museum at Gettysburg filled with artifacts about the battle. Little did Cliff know that he would someday be the grandfather/patriarch of a whole bunch of later Arquettes who also would make their marks in the acting business.

So many great personalities guested on the Ford Show with us and left memories that will last forever, like ... :

Western character actor Andy Devine - who made us laugh when he told Dean and me in his gravelly voice that we should enlist in the submarine branch of the US Navy, because, if we were torpedoed, we'd die quickly with very little pain ...

Movie tough-guys George Raft and Peter Lorré - contrary to image - both truly "*gentle*"-men ... pussycats! ...

Joe E. Brown, with his super-big-sized mouth and matching big heart, reminding us, as he said in "Some Like It Hot," "Well, nobody's perfect" ...

Phyllis Diller, madcap wacko extraordinaire, who kept making me the welcome butt of her jokes as she did a whole number on my then-skinny appearance ...

Harold Lloyd, the daring clock-hand-hanging silent screen comic, pulling off a glove to show me how a movie-explosion-gone-wrong years ago had blown off some of his fingers ...

Charles Schultz, just as gentle as the "Peanuts" characters he drew, wearing a sweater that could have been stolen from Charlie Brown himself ...

Willie Mays, the "Say-Hey Kid," comfortable fingering the San Francisco Giants baseball he brought with him to the studio, but very ill at ease at the questions tossed to him ...

Ted Lewis, with his battered top hat and vaudeville banter of another era, regaling us with his signature songs "When My Baby Smiles At Me," and "Me And My Shadow" and then yelling at the lighting man when the spotlight missed him ...

Veteran English character actor Terry-Thomas, who arrived to amuse us wearing a bright canary yellow suit and possessing a gap in his front teeth big enough to house the entire British navy ...

Hermoine Gingold, the character actress's character actress, who arrived at the studio with her own personal "Gay

Mafia" of fawners and gofers and charmed us all with her raised eyebrows and biting wit ...

Merle Oberon, forever "Cathy" in Samuel Goldwyn's "Wuthering Heights," still a great beauty even in her fifties and attracting the eye and interest of every man in the studio ...

Helen Hayes, the first lady of the American theater, so very regal in her quiet demeanor that she could indeed have been a real queen herself ...

Richard Nixon - always running for office even when he wasn't; shaking every audience member's hand, trying *so* hard to be just one of the gang (but blowing it by calling Ernie by the wrong nickname: "You Old "*Bean*picker" instead of "*Pea*picker") ...

And Robert Kennedy - frailer and shorter than I thought he'd be, surrounded by Secret Service Men who followed him even into the bathroom! I possess a collection of old TV kinescopes of the "Ernie Ford Show," and the one I'm proudest of is the Bobby Kennedy appearance in 1963, some months before his brother was assassinated. Ernie explained to the Attorney General that Dean and I were both students at Stanford and San Jose State and that this was our first national show, to which Mr. Kennedy replied, "They're VERY good!" I treasure that.

Dean and I certainly should have received an diploma in music education from the wealth of talent who blessed "The Tennessee Ernie Ford Show." A history of jazz could have been filmed, just based on some of our guests. We had Meade "Lux" Lewis playing his trademark barrel house piano, Lionel Hampton knocking us out with his dynamite personality and swinging vibes, Turk Murphy blowing his patented "San Francisco" brand of Dixieland, Earl "Fatha" Hines rockin' the joint with his legendary piano, and Erroll Garner sitting on a borrowed telephone book on the piano bench playing his composition "Misty" for us all. George Shearing also showed up on the Ford Show with his guide dog who was happily content to listen to his master play while curling up under the piano (the dog, not Shearing). Some ten years later, I saw George Shearing do a marvelous turn at a jazz club in Hollywood. I must preface this by saying one of the kings of jazz piano is a black artist also named "Hank Jones," whose ASCAP checks I sometime receive and vice versa. After Shearing, who is sightless, finished his lovely set, I went backstage to offer my congratulations to him.

I knocked on his dressing room door, was welcomed inside, and introduced myself by saying, "Hi George - I'm Hank Jones" - to which Mr. Shearing replied, "No you're not!"

Other musical bases were covered well by some of our other guests. In the Gospel arena, we had Clara Ward and her Gospel Pearls, Hovie Lister and the Statesmen Quartet, Elvis's Jordanaires, and JD Sumner with the Blackwood Brothers. In country music, we were entertained by Homer & Jethro, Lester Flatt and Earl Scruggs, and Little Jimmy Dickens (who relished showing us the scratches on his back given by a passionate one-night-stand the night before). 50s and 60s pop artists who were fun to get to know included Bobby Rydell - a really talented nice kid, Gisele MacKenzie who played a mean violin too, Gogi Grant who told us about "The Wayward Wind," the Chordettes who confided that "Ernie was so much nicer than Arthur Godfrey," Frankie Laine who took us on a ride on the "Mule Train" and warned us against "Jezebel," Jack Scott who reminded us that "She Was My True Love," Buddy Greco who showed us why "The Lady Is A Tramp," the Paris Sisters who told how "I Love How You Love Me," and Johnny Tillotson who sang of "Poetry In Motion." Those memories sure haunt the corners of my (now-fading) mind.

Appearing on television 5-days-week in homes across America ensured more RCA Victor recording dates. In January 1962, Neely Plumb called us to come down and record some of our own tunes for potential singles release. Once again using Jimmy Haskell's arrangements, we cut "Train-Train-Train," "Ain't Got A Nickel," "Wishin' Well, and another version of "I'm Gonna Build Myself A Raft," this time featuring James Burton more prominently on guitar. They turned out well, and the RCA brass then okayed us recording an entire album. It was called "Arrival Time" and featured a mix of our own songs ("Let It Happen Again," Who's It Gonna' Be,?" a raucous version of "Billy Boy," and others) plus some standards that were now part of our act ("Long, Long Trail," "A Lovely Way To Spend An Evening," "Sing Boy Sing," "Ivory Tower," Dean really wailing on "Sentimental Journey," and me crooning on "Harbor Lights," among others. It received a "Billboard Pick" evaluation in that music magazine, their review saying "(Hank & Dean's) blend is unusual and their style is fresh and imaginative. Talented lads should go far."

In between tapings of the Ford Show, our label sent us out to the hinterlands to promote our records. On Thanksgiving weekend in 1962, we flew to Philadelphia to appear with Dick Clark on his highly-successful "American Bandstand." It was a wild experience because every high school kid who danced on the show had their very own fan club themselves and was more camera-savvy than *we* were. Coming out of the ABC studio in Philly, we ran into Tony Bennett doing some promotion for his own platters on Columbia. He did a take as he saw us and then gave me a wink. I knew where that wink came from: George Burke used to book the Fairmount Hotel in San Francisco, and in 1961 we were George's guests at Tony's opening there. At that particular performance, Bennett introduced a new song that had never been heard before - a song about "little cable cars climbing halfway to the stars" and how "the morning fog will chill the air ..." Afterwards, Tony joined us at our table and asked us what we thought of his new song. Everyone chimed in that they thought "I Left My Heart In San Francisco" was going to be a real winner - except ME. I told Tony Bennett that, while I thought it was a pretty tune, it's appeal was too localized to probably ever be a big national hit. Thus, the wink. Can I pick 'em or what!!?? Flying home from the Bandstand appearance, we had to contend with and then comfort the flight attendant in the First Class Cabin who was crying up a storm about being away from her family and missing them over Turkey-Day. We didn't mind - hey, we got on "Bandstand," didn't we?

We went lots of other places too. We judged beauty contests and talent shows throughout the west coast. We winged to Baltimore to do radio shows with hot jocks like "Fat Daddy," sharing the green room with an up and coming act called "Patti LaBelle & The Blubells." We did record hops in the midwest, appearing at dances with Elvis sound-a-like Ral Donner and Bobby Hatfield and Bill Medley, The Righteous Brothers. We traveled to Salt Lake City where we joined fellow RCA artist Michael Landon, then on "Bonanza," in opening a record store there and signing our names on the establishment's wall (it's still there, some 45 years later). I remember Mike wanted a *real* drink in dry Salt Lake City, so we went down to the basement of the record distributorship there. The RCA guy smuggled in a bottle for "Little Joe" and some cokes for us. Then on another trip, we flew up to Portland, Oregon to appear as special guests at their Rose Festival there with Connie Stevens. I remember that one especially well because that's where we met a couple who would become life-long friends, Bob Adkins - "Addie Bobkins" on Portland's most popular and zany children's show - and his beautiful wife Joanne.

One RCA excursion still provokes laughs as I think about it. We went to Chicago to push "Arrival Time" on an itinerary planned and hosted by their record distributor there. Little did we know that that RCA branch in the Windy City was sort of controlled by, how you say, "the mob." A bunch of wise guys took us to the best Italian restaurant in town and told us to order anything we wanted. The head guy's "date" for the evening was a clinging peroxide blonde in a dress tighter than tight. Trying to impress his two college-boy guests and be on his best behavior, Mr. Soprano, or whatever his name was, turned to his date, pointed to the menu, and inquired, "And what will the lovely broad have?" We tried to stifle our laughter because we felt that - if we even cracked a smile - we'd be rubbed out.

On that same trip, we went on Chicago's popular "Marty Faye TV Show" to plug our album. Other guests on that program included jazz greats Dizzy Gillespie, Ben Webster, and Joe Williams. Dizzy especially was a wonder, sly like a fox in his humor and playing music from almost another dimension compared to everyone else. In a move that ranks with us singing "Jailhouse Rock" at Santa Rita Prison Farm, Dean and I chose to entertain on that show with our white-bread version of the old black work-song "Pick A Bale Of Cotton." I'll never forget the expressions on Dizzy and Joe's faces as we sang of how we used to toil day and night in the cotton fields: it ranked with the response the opening night audience gave when they first heard "Springtime For Hitler" in Mel Brooks's "The Producers." Oh God - WHAT were we thinking???

More recording sessions followed on RCA. In July of 1962, we cut some sides with Jack Nitsche as arranger, just to get a different sound from the many we had recorded with Jimmy Haskell (Jack had done lots of jobs for Phil Spector and later was to go on and arrange for The Rolling Stones and Neil Young). Our plug side was the old Burton Lane - Yip Harburg standard "Old Devil Moon," modernized and made more upbeat by Nitsche with horns, guitars, and a girl chorus. *Variety* gave the platter a "Best Bet - Top Single of the Week" review, saying

"Hank Jones & Dean Kay's 'Old Devil Moon' dishes up this great show-tune with a modern beat and an arresting sound which should give it a potent spinning lift." It did receive some airplay around the nation backed with country writer Harlan Howard's "And They Did" on the flip side, but never really took off. Some thirty years later, Dean played our record of "Old Devil Moon" for its composer and his fellow ASCAP Board member Burton Lane to see what he thought of our version of his song. Mr. Lane pronounced it "terrible."

In late 1963, RCA Victor released us from our contract. Our records had made some noise, but didn't engender enough sales really to persuade the company to pick up our option. I guess you could say that we sold to some of our Ford Show fans, but didn't break out beyond that group. What's funny today is that some of our old RCA discs pop up on the web for sale to 60s record buffs. Our "Arrival Time" album was recently listed for sale on a site for $58.00. Where were they when we *needed* them??

George Burke then engineered a deal for us with Bob Keene's Del Fi Record label. It was a small company, but had had huge hits with Ritchie Valens, Johnny Crawford, and some black r&b artists. Under Keene's direction, we recorded a single called "Rosanna" backed by the superb playing of Glen Campbell on twelve-string guitar. Keene on Del Fi was able to pull a much more commercial sound from us than Neely did on RCA. But just as the record was ready to be released, Uncle Sam called ... for Dean.

Ah, timing! Dean ended up having to serve six months active duty in the military and then time in the reserves. But Ernie had hired a singing *team* and needed two voices for the hymns, so we reluctantly had to leave the Ford Show. They gave us a good sendoff on our last program. I remember it well because I blubbered on the air saying goodbye to our TV family.

For the next two years, we guested on the Ford Show every so often once Dean could be available again. It was great coming home. We kept in touch with the rest of the cast and crew over the years, most all of who remain now lifelong pals. Dick Noel, "Old Silver Throat," went back to Chicago where he became a huge success in the voice-over field there. He moved to San Diego in the 80s with his wife Nancy, and today I count them both among my best friends in the world; they were the ones who introduced me to my wife Bonnie. Dick has produced my last six albums which were released on his Epitomé Records label. Anita Gordon, our "girl singer," remarried and moved to the Orient. Jim Lange, our announcer on the Ford Show, had great success as host of "The Dating Game" on TV and today is one of the San Francisco Bay Area's top radio personalities. Jack Fascinato, our musical conductor, continued on working with Ernie but later was diagnosed with Alzheimer's disease. Although he lost his ability to recognize family and friends, Jack still retained his amazing musicianship and, even in the worst phases of his disease, could play most any song on the piano when requested to do so. Of the production staff and crew, I still am in contact with Bill Martin, John Inzerella, Don "SJ" Gold, Dave Seely, Jack Van Scyoc, Ernie's manager Jim Loakes and his agent Dale Sheets among others.

Ernie continued to perform. In the 70s, I went to the California State Fair where he was headlining. When I went backstage to say "hi," Ernie greeted me warmly and said, tongue in cheek, "Oh Hank, if I'd have known you were out there, I would have been so nervous - I never could have gone on." Right! In his later years, he lived in Portola Valley in the hills behind my old alma mater, Stanford University. In his semi-retirement, the Old Peapicker often would drop in at the neighborhood garden and hardware store, wearing his old jeans and Pendleton shirt. He'd casually take out his pipe, and then proceed to work behind the counter all day, showing surprised customers where to find seeds, manure, and the latest tools. He remained just "one of the guys" to the end. Just before his death in 1991, Dean and I got a chance to visit with him again, when the Nashville Network celebrated his 50th anniversary in show business with a TV special. Dinah Shore, George Gobel, Della Reese, Don & Phil Everly, Molly Bee, dear Minnie Pearl and many more all showed up to honor our friend. It was a wonderful experience, because we had a chance to sort of "close the circle." When the three of us posed for a picture together, Ernie winked and smiled, saying, "Well, here we are again after all these years ... the famous team of 'Art, Bart, and Fargo!'"

I was proud to be a member of his team, and I miss Tennessee Ernie Ford very much.

JOIN OL'ERN AND HIS GANG IN THEIR SAN FRANCISCO STUDIO

Ernie has fun with the audience prior to his ABC-TV daytime show.

Ernie's gang: Standing-from left: Jim Lange, Anita Gordon, Jack Fascinato, Dean Kay; Seated-from left: Dick Noel, Ernie and Hank Jones.

FREE TICKETS!

To visit The Ernie Ford Show in San Francisco, simply fill out and mail the back page of this folder. Your free tickets will be mailed promptly.

WESTERN UNION
TELEGRAM
W. P. MARSHALL, PRESIDENT

1201 (4-00)

The filing time shown in the date line on domestic telegrams is LOCAL TIME at point of origin. Time of receipt is 1962 APR 2 AM 9 05 point of destination

OA017 SSE067

O SFC220 (PB094 YRG002) PD=DCTL YRG NEW YORK NY 2 1045A EST=

HANK JONES AND DEAN KAY ABC-TV STUDIOS=

TENNESSEE ERNIE SHOW SFRAN=

BEST TO YOU FROM ALL OF US HERE AT RCA VICTOR, YOUR
RECORDING OF "WISHIN' WELL" GOES OUT NEXT WEEK. KNOW YOU
HAVE A WONDERFUL FUTURE IN SHOW BUSINESS=

ROBERT L YORKE DIVISION VICE PRES COMMERCIAL RECORDS
CREATION DEPT.=

Congratulations

1962 APR 2 PM 12 06

OA113 LB2 68

L HDA112 CGN PD=FAM HOLLYWOOD CALIF 2 0100A PST=

HANK JONES AND DEAN KAY=

560 HAAS AVE SAN LEANDRO CALIF=

WARMEST CONGRATULATIONS ON YOUR OPENING SHOW AND MAY IT
BE THE FIRST OF A LONG STRING OF SUCCESSES=
STEVE SHOLES AND THE RCA VICTOR GANG.

HANK JONES, ERNIE FORD, & DEAN KAY, 1962

SINGING THE CLOSING HYMN
ERNIE FORD. DEAN KAY. HANK JONES. & DICK NOEL

HANK JONES, ERNIE FORD, & DEAN KAY

HANK JONES, MINNIE PEARL (sans make-up), DEAN KAY,
ANITA GORDON, DICK NOEL, ERNIE FORD, & JIM LANGE

1215

[NAME]

is a member in good standing of the

OFFICIAL

Hank Jones & Dean Kay

FAN CLUB

_____CHAPTER

[CHAPTER NAME]

APPROVED BY

George R. Burke

PERSONAL MANAGER OF
HANK JONES & DEAN KAY

"OLD SILVER-THROAT" DICK NOEL TEACHES HANK & DEAN
THE FINE POINTS OF GROUP SINGING - 1962

HANK JONES, CONNIE STEVENS, DEAN KAY
PORTLAND ROSE FESTIVAL SPECIAL GUESTS, 1963

HANK JONES & DEAN KAY WITH THE LEGENDARY BLACKWOOD BROTHERS GOSPEL GROUP - 1963
WITH FORD SHOW ORCHESTRA LEADER JACK FASCINATO (RT.) & ELVIS'S BASS SINGER JD SUMMER (TOP RT.)

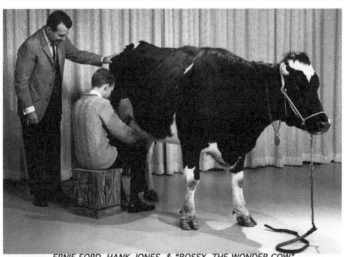

ERNIE FORD, HANK JONES, & "BOSSY, THE WONDER COW"
1963

HANK JONES, ANITA GORDON, DEAN KAY, ERNIE FORD, & BOB HOPE
"THE TENNESSEE ERNIE FORD SHOW," ABC-TV, 1962

Ringiers Unterhaltungs-Blätter
«Das gelbe Heft»
Nr. 39

Hank und Dean bestreiten singend ihr Studium

GET OUT YOUR SAURKRAUT -
HANK & DEAN WERE THE BEST-WURST IN GERMANY!

HANK JONES

A Rock 'n' Rolling Genealogist

Hank, a baritone, rehearses with buddy Dean Kay, tenor, at least three hours a day besides taping and rehearsing the Tennessee Ernie Ford show three days a week. Research in genealogy is also a daily pastime

DEAN KAY, HANK JONES, STEPHANIE HILL, RICHARD EGAN, MAX BAER JR.
ABC-TV PRESS PARTY, OCTOBER 1962

HANK JONES, NICK ADAMS, DEAN JONES, STEPHANIE HILL, & DEAN KAY
PRESS PARTY FOR ALL NEW ABC-TV SHOWS, 1962

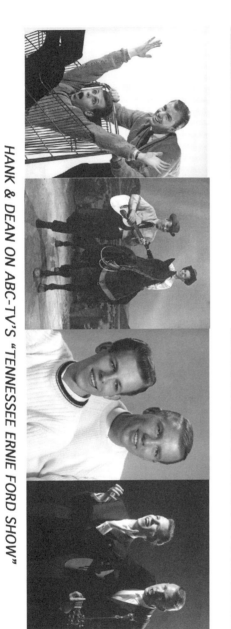

BetFord CORPORATION   Producers of "THE TENNESSEE ERNIE FORD SHOW"

645 LARKIN STREET • SAN FRANCISCO 9, CALIFORNIA • PROSPECT 1-0670

WILLIAM N. BURCH
Producer-Director

Dear Hank and Dean –

I just want you both to once again know how very much I personally appreciate your great contribution to our show.

As we come to the end of the first "260" -- I can only say I'm looking forward to the next "520" with more than passive enthusiasm -- due in no small part to your fine talent and co.operation. Bless you!

I like you too —

Ernie

TELEVISION CROSSWORD

ACROSS

1 Creeping vine
7 Comic Joe E. ___
12 Joey on *Fury*
14 *Wide Country* locale
15 Enemy agent
16 Actress Dolores
   Del ___
17 Tal in *Empire*
18 Stars in 14 Across
20 Sign of a hit show
   (abbreviation)
21 John McIntire's role
23 Window frame
25 *All Star* ___
26 Plagued
30 Arabian chief
31 Skelton's music man
32 ___ ___ the *Truth*
   (2 words)
35 Point of time
36 Hank and Dean
38 Mellow
39 Exclamation of
   surprise
42 Mel in *The Dick
   Van Dyke Show*
44 Producer Susskind
46 O'Toole's notebook
47 One of the Gabor
   sisters
50 Wife in *Our Man
   Higgins*
51 Beaver's surname
53 French sculptor
54 He's McHale

See next week's TV GUIDE for solution

DICK NOEL & BILL MARTIN WITH THEIR FABLED "SCREW"

"TENNESSEE ERNIE FORD SHOW REUNION" – 1980'S
TOLUCA LAKE, CALIFORNIA

DIZZY GILLESPIE, JOE WILLIAMS, & HANK & DEAN
THE MARTY FAYE SHOW, CHICAGO, 1963

STAN LAUREL

One day on the "Tennessee Ernie Ford" program, Ernie asked the cast, "Of all the great people in history, who would you like to spend an hour with, if you had the chance?" Dean said, "Abraham Lincoln." Dick Noel reflected and answered, "Leonardo DaVinci." Our announcer Jim Lange thought and replied "Beethoven." And I said, very seriously, ... "Stan Laurel." I'd been a lifelong fan of Oliver Hardy's skinny partner and considered him the funniest man ever to grace the silver screen.

Well, guess what? I was the only person on the show who got his wish. (DaVinci, Lincoln, and Beethoven were unavailable). Stan heard about my response, and we started a correspondence that lasted several years. In his many letters, he generously gave me performance tips and commiserated about the feast or famine aspects of show business when I was "between pictures" (which was often!). And then one day in late 1964, out of the blue, I received a phone call:

"Hello, lad," said a soft, unmistakable English voice. "Come on over, let's have a visit."

What an afternoon we spent. He lived in a smallish Santa Monica apartment, filled with a lifetime's worth of memorabilia. Stan was much more outgoing and gregarious than his timid character on screen. His eyes twinkled with good humor, and he had the most marvelous belly-laugh - so contagious, you couldn't help but join in. He was the *real* director of the Laurel and Hardy films. They were largely formed from his inspiration and comic genius. I had a ball picking his brain for answers to questions I'd wondered about for years. Stan enthralled me with stories about how he and Charlie Chaplin came to America on a cattle boat together as members of an English Music Hall troupe. And he let me in on some of the technical secrets that helped their film gags come off so well.

I WAS IN HEAVEN!

One thing that struck me was his genuine modesty. Stan was absolutely amazed at how many people around the world seemed to love him. He showed me his new color television set, sent as a gift anonymously with a note attached from "just a fan who wants to say thanks for all the laughter you've given us."

And the stories he told! He related how one time after they retired from films, he and Oliver Hardy were making a tour of Europe and docked at Cobh, Ireland. He said there were hundreds of boats blowing whistles, and mobs of people screaming on the docks. Laurel and Hardy thought, at first, all the commotion was for someone else on board the ship - royalty, maybe. They just couldn't understand what all the ruckus was about. But then, Stan said, something happened that they never forgot: All the church bells in that little Irish town started to ring out the Laurel and Hardy movie theme, the "Cuckoo Song," as the crowd below sang along and cheered. He looked at Hardy, Ollie looked back at him - and they both cried.

That wonderful afternoon went on and on. I thought I might tire him out (he already had suffered two strokes previously and had a bad heart condition). But Stan insisted I stay and talk some more. Finally, it was time to leave. As we said our farewells, he said cryptically to me, "Well, Hank, the next time you see me - I'll have 'me hat on." I really didn't know what he meant, but I smiled and said goodbye.

Ten weeks later, Stan Laurel was dead.

A few months after his passing, I was watching an old Laurel and Hardy short subject at home on television. In one scene, he and Oliver were preparing to be hanged for some offense relating to their glorious ineptitude. But they were both concerned that they wouldn't be able to recognize one another and be buddies when they finally got to heaven.

And then, in the movie, Stan said something that sent chills up my spine. He consoled his friend by telling him, "Don't worry, Ollie, you'll know me up there ... when you see me, ... "*I'll have 'me hat on*!"

I paid my initial respects to Stan at his viewing at Forest Lawn Cemetery. It was really strange to see him in his coffin, as I'd just been with him but a few weeks before when he was so vital and full of spunk. The embalmer had taken years off him with whatever cosmetic work he did, and he uncannily looked in death like the Stan Laurel of the 1920s silent film days. Lois Laurel, his daughter - later to become a good friend, was there making funeral arrangements. Just as I was about to leave, there was a phone call for Lois. The mortician handed her the telephone saying, "Mr. Charles Chaplin is calling from Switzerland." After years of some estrangement, the "Little Tramp," himself now aged and infirm, was making one last effort to reach out to his old English Music-Hall friend. It was hard for me to hold back my tears - I felt I was so privileged to be eavesdropping on a part of history.

Stan's funeral was lovely - a true celebration of his life. Dick Van Dyke gave a marvelous eulogy, the thrust of which was when anyone had a problem or was in doubt about how to make something funny – all they had to do was "just ask Stan." At the close of the service, the organ and the bells once again rang out "The Cuckoo Song," as they had years before when Stan and Babe Hardy visited that little town in Ireland. There wasn't a dry eye in the house. So many of his old friends from Hal Roach Studios were there, like Andy Clyde, Allan Mowbray, and Patsy Kelly, plus all the behind-the-scenes crew who had worked along side him for years. All through the service, I was sitting next to a small, bald-headed man with a sad and woebegone face. When I walked outside the church, the little fellow asked if I knew what time it was. Only then did I recognize him and realize that I had been sitting next to Buster Keaton at Stan Laurel's funeral. That's something I'll tell my grandchildren about someday.

Some months after Stan's death, Mrs. Laurel sent my name on to Bill Patterson, Grand Sheik of the "Way Out West Tent" of the Laurel & Hardy film buff's club "Sons of the Desert" as one who should be a prospective member. It was a great group of guys and gals whose one common bond was a deep love for "The Boys." We would meet once a month to toast Stan and Babe, enjoy their films, and meet show-folk who had once worked with them in years past. On our stationary, we honored them with their likenesses with the caption underneath, "Two minds without a single thought!" We opened each meeting singing as they did in their movie,

"We are the Sons Of The Desert - having the time
of our lives, marching along, two thousand
strong, far from our sweethearts and wives - God
Bless them."

We often would be accompanied on piano by T. Marvin Hatley, who had composed the music to that classic comedy as well near hundreds of others.

I was elected Grand Sheik of Sons of the Desert myself and served several years. My then-wife Lori was a driving force in running the club, and much of its success was due to her hard work over many years. It was so neat to get to know some of the cast and crew of the Laurel & Hardy pictures who were so instrumental in making them so funny and endure even to this day. Guests often included some of their co-stars like Sheila Ryan, Billy Bletcher, Henry Brandon - the wicked villain "Silas Barnaby" from "Babes in Toyland", and the marvelous Anita Garvin. People who had worked with them on USO tours also showed up: I was awakened one early Sunday morning by a phone call from the great Ray Bolger who just wanted to chat and tell me his fond reminisces of camp shows with Stan and Babe during the war; the Wizard Of Oz's "Scarecrow" went on and on about how much he loved "The Boys." Among many others who attended our meetings were perpetual fans like producer Jay Ward, actor Charles Martin Smith, teacher Bob Satterfield, artist Larry Byrd, animator Earl Kress, comic Chuck McCann, L&H author Randy Skretvedt, and my dear pal comedy-writer Paul Pumpian, as well as Roach behind-the-scenes people like optical effects expert Roy Seawright and director George Marshall. Add to this several of Stan's wives like Virginia Ruth Laurel and Ida Laurel (never to be invited to the same meeting, of course), Stan's daughter Lois Laurel Brooks and her husbands Rand Brooks and Tony Hawes, and Babe Hardy's widow Lucille and her second husband Ben Price, and you can be sure that we had some great get-togethers.

Billy Gilbert, who was their chief foil in many of the L&H pictures including their Oscar-winning short "The Music Box," came to a couple of meetings. His trademark used to be his comic sneezes which he performed with all kinds of nuances and variations. Sadly, in his later years, Billy suffered a stroke or two that impaired his ability to execute his "achoos." But at the meetings, his strong-willed wife sternly ordered him to "sneeze, Billy ... come-on, SNEEZE!," hitting him on the nose like you would a Pekingese dog to make him perform, and Billy came through with some pips that rivaled his classics from the old days.

At one of our yearly banquets, we had as our honored guest Hal Roach, who had produced all the best Laurel & Hardy movies, as well as creating the "Our Gang/Little Rascals" series and films for Harold Lloyd, Harry Langdon, Charlie Chase and so many others in the pioneer years of Hollywood. We engineered a meeting between Billy Gilbert and Hal Roach who had not seen each other probably since the 1930s. When ailing Billy saw Mr. Roach walk in the door, he struggled to his feet from his chair and leaned on his cane for support. With his eyes watering and his lips quivering, the great comic emotionally greeted his old boss with, "MISTER Roach, oh MISTER Roach - it's SO good to see you again ... after all these years." Billy looked at me and said, "This is the Master ... This is the Master." Hal Roach, who was a pretty steely old guy, was greatly moved by this reception and said " Billy ... Billy ... it's good to see you too. Sit down, Billy - sit down." The legacy that these two men left was very evident and appreciated by all who attended that night, as we laughed ourselves silly looking at some of the short subjects that their combined genius had produced.

Hal Roach was a true head of a motion picture studio. You knew it, because he rarely used the word "I" - as in "I did this." He spoke about himself in the third person and would say instead, "Roach did this," talking about himself. Damnedest thing I ever heard. He and Stan Laurel had a sort of love-hate relationship because Stan insisted on calling the shots on the L&H films, and Roach felt *he* was the one who should be in control. But at the banquet Roach was gracious and appreciative of Stan's talents and said so. He even had a bit of ham in him still himself (he and Harold Lloyd had started together in the silents as film extras) and insisted on entertaining the banquet crowd with what he called "the lazy man's hula." Hal Roach lived past his 100th birthday and was honored by emcee Billy Crystal at the Oscars just prior to his passing. After being introduced, Hal Roach, unfortunately unmiked, launched into a lengthy but inaudible monologue from the audience, prompting Crystal to ad-lib: "Seems appropriate that he got his start in silent films."

Another one of our memorable banquets was a salute to surviving members of another Roach series, the "Our Gang" kids. What a treat it was to see them all together again. Stymie Beard arrived complete with his derby and cane, bringing with him the lead singer of the singing group The Platters who serenaded us by crooning his big hit "Only You." Sunshine Sammy Morrison and Dorothy DeBorba from the earliest "Our Gang" regaled us with memories of the group's formative years in the 20s. Dear Darla Hood, still such a sweetheart, endeared herself to us all with her lovely smile and gentle ways. Tommy "Butch" Bond, the perennial bully, kidded around giving us menacing looks and glares. And George "Spanky" MacFarland sauntered in, cocky and confident as ever - just like when he was a kid, wearing his trademarked plaid cap for all to see. Spanky joined us at our table for dinner that night, and it was amazing to see how little he had changed in attitude from the days when he and Alfalfa Switzer were truly little rascals.

Babe London was often a guest at the meetings and then at our home for Thanksgiving dinner every year. She played "the fat girl" in many silents and early talkies, including "A Day's Pleasure" with Charlie Chaplin and "Our Wife," with Laurel & Hardy. Babe resided out in Woodland Hills at the Motion Picture Country Home, and I would visit her often there. It was such fun to meet some of her fellow residents such as Mary Astor, the femme fatale in "The Maltese Falcon," Larry Fine of the Three Stooges, and Chester Conklin of Mack Sennett's Keystone Cops; Johnny Weissmuller, movie's favorite "Tarzan," was in a wheel chair and would scoot around the Country Home halls giving his famous Tarzan yell and scaring everybody he met as he tried to run them over. On the door of her cottage at the Home, Babe had a little sign that said "Expect a miracle." She had a contagious positive outlook that made her a joy to be around.

I often would escort Babe to show-business functions as her "date." One time we went to a taping of the Merv Griffin Show where Babe was featured with other stars from the silent days and then on to a cocktail party afterwards hosted by the convivial Merv. I was in awe when I met the legendary Lillian Gish, who had been part of movie history from D. W. Griffith and "Birth of a Nation" on. She was so sweet and kind, very ladylike. Thanks to Babe, I also had a chance to rub shoulders with some early silent stars whose names now are only memories to a few: Betty Blythe (the "Queen of Sheba"), Charles "Buddy" Rogers (from the first Oscar winning movie "Wings," husband of Mary Pickford), Richard Arlen, Jackie Coogan ("The Kid" with Chaplin, later "Uncle Fester" on TV's "The Addams Family"), and Minta Durfee Arbuckle (widow of the legendary Fatty A. of scandal fame). Betty Bronson, so memorable as "Peter Pan" in the 20s with whom I appeared in "Blackbeard's Ghost" in the 60s, was also there, and it was good to see her again.

On another evening, I was Babe's escort at a big Motion Picture Relief Fund Gala at the Music Center downtown. We had box seats and enjoyed superb entertainment provided by (and wait until you hear THIS bill): Bob Hope, Mitzi Gaynor, Pearl

Bailey, The 5th Dimension, Jack Benny, Barbra Streisand, and Frank Sinatra. It was hosted by Princess Grace of Monaco, Cary Grant, Jimmy Stewart, Gregory Peck, and Rosalind Russell. With all these star-power names knocking us out with their talents, in a million years you'd never guess who absolutely stole the show: Jimmy Durante! I've never in my life seen a performer who engendered so much laughter and pure love from his audience. "The Schnoz" was magnificent from his rousing opening of "Inka-Dinka-Doo" until he said goodnight to Mrs. Calabash.

Sons of the Desert was and is a great group. It reinforced what Stan told us:

"You can lead a horse to water ... but a pencil must be led."

I've lived by that!

My friendship with Stan Laurel also led to one of the most moving encounters I've ever had. In the late 70s, there was an article in the Calendar Section of the L.A. Times about those comics who had been influential in making Las Vegas thrive in its formative years. The usual group was mentioned like Jerry Lewis, Shecky Greene, Jan Murray, Don Rickles and others. Then in the Calendar "Letters To The Editor" section the following week was a letter written from prison by black comedian George Kirby who was serving time there for a drug bust. He had reached the heights of the entertainment world - even having his own TV show - but was brought crashing down by his severe addiction. In the letter, Kirby commended those named in the article, but closed with, "Doesn't anyone remember George Kirby as breaking new ground in Vegas in the early days too?"

I felt his response was so poignant and sad that I wrote George a note at his prison. I told him that I had seen him perform in Vegas some years before as opening act for Petula Clark, and that he had knocked me out with his hilarious impressions and comedy material. I stressed that in no way was he forgotten. In the original article Kirby had also mentioned that he himself had been influenced as a young man by Laurel & Hardy's movies. So, along with my letter to him, I decided to enclose some issues of the Way Out West Tent's publication *Pratfall*, our little magazine dedicated to Stan and Babe and their films. George and I then began a long correspondence back and forth about Laurel & Hardy and show-business in general. I kept on sending him articles about "The Boys" and their behind-the-scenes secrets of how they made certain gags work in their films. It turned out George loved the duo just as much as I did. We developed a really close bond via the U.S. mails thanks to our mutual affection for Laurel & Hardy. He even wrote that he had my family's picture posted on his cell wall.

When he was released from prison, a small notice in the newspaper reported that George Kirby would be making his first post-prison personal appearance at a small nightclub down in Long Beach. I decided to go and show some support for my pen-pal. The club was in a seedy area of town and when I entered I wasn't so sure it was safe to be there. Then all my concerns were forgotten when George came on and blew us away with his sensational material and his still-perfect timing. He hadn't lost a thing from his long imprisonment. He even did a heartrending self-written song called "King Heroin," about the deadly drug that had pulled him down. After his act was completed, George received a well-deserved standing ovation. He was back.

I wasn't so sure if I should, but I went backstage anyway just to shake his hand and tell him I enjoyed the show. When I arrived in his dressing room, he was surrounded by well-wishers who felt the same way. I kind of hung back until they all had cleared out and then cautiously walked up to him. All I said was, "Hi George, I'm Hank Jones." There was a long pause as he looked at me with a riveting gaze. Then with tears streaming down his cheeks, George Kirby held open his arms and hugged me with the tightest hug I've ever had. He wouldn't let go - he just wouldn't let go. He squeezed and squeezed for what seemed like forever. All he said finally was, "Thank you ... thank you, Hank."

I treasure that special moment probably as much as any other moment in my entire life. And it would not have happened had it not been for a gentle man from Ulverston, England named Stan Laurel.

STAN LAUREL
(1890 - 1965)

JAN. 29th.'65.

Thanks Hank, yours, 27th.inst.with enclosure TV
Guide clipping re Skelton program Feb.2nd.Appreciate
the reminder,shall watch with interest.I too saw
Gracie Fields on the Paar show - she certainly has
aged,but I enjoyed seeing her again. Sorry business
is slow,unfortunately its always that way BETWEEN
PICTURES is'nt it??!!   Take care of yourself Hank -

         as always -

                    Stan

              STAN LAUREL.

STAN LAUREL
849 OCEAN AVENUE
SANTA MONICA, CALIFORNIA
ZIP CODE 90403

SEPT.19th.'64.

Dear Hank Jones:
              Many thanks your very nice letter
of July 16th.ult. Appreciate very much your kind
sentiments so warmly expressed also the compliment
you paid me on the 'Ernie Ford'Show - am afraid
I would be very disappointing in a discussion on
Comedy - something I prefer not to be questioned -
even EINSTEIN would be baffled.!
          Wish you a happy & successful career in Show
Bus. its a rough old Road Hank - need lots of
courage & fortitude to survive.
              Good luck - God Bless.

                         as always -

                    Stan Laurel.

                 STAN LAUREL.

SOME NOTES FROM STAN

Fred Karno's "SKATING" the film title was "The Rink", another one was "THE SHOW" (Night in an English Music Hall").

The "Music Hall" is no more in England - completely vanished - same as the old American Vaudeville - a tragic situation for show Bus. we've lost a great school of training unfortunately.

Yes Beatrice Lillie is a great example of that thorough training a wonderful personality - she's "TIFFANY".

Nice to hear from you again Hank.

Take care - God Bless.

as always -

Stan

STAN LAUREL.

---

849 OCEAN AVENUE
SANTA MONICA, CALIF.
OCT.14th.'64.

Dear Hank Jones:

Thanks yours,13th.inst.

Sorry to tell you,Jimmy Finlayson passed on in 1953. he only worked occasionally for a few years previous due to ill health. Re your questions "Night in an English Music Hall', can only answer these briefly,otherwise take to long.

1. It was produced originally in England by Fred Karno early 1900's. So successful, Karno formed several troupes to play in different Countries,one Co.played on the Continent,France, Germany etc. two in England -- the London troupe & the American Provincial, & the American Troupe. It was'nt a Revue,just a 30 minute vaudeville act.I4 in the Co. many doubling in parts & audience characters sitting in the 'BOXES', (stage on a stage,a proscenium arch,front heavy drapes & on each side 2 or 4 private boxes - this was the set as the regular theatre audience viewed it from in front. of the regular orchestra pit. A typical English Music Hall show was presented with 6 acts of dubious talent - each was resented & insulted by a white tie 'DRUNK'- he several times climbed out of the box & took part in the show. It was a terrific hit in the States from Coast to Coast in vaudeville also played a season with Ziegfeld Follies - the late Billy Reeves played the Drunk - the Chaplin troupe was the last to Come over (I think we were the 6th. & last Co.) then Chaplin left the Co. to join Mack Sennett Studio in 1913. the troupe finally disbanned. I remained & continued working in vaudeville.

2. Several of the Karno boys appeared on the screen - BILLY RITCHIE made a few Silent films, also a JIMMY AUBREY - SYD CHAPLIN (Charlie's Brother) but never became prominent. Karno only visited America,was never a permanent resident.

3. I never worked with Chaplin in films - I seldom saw him ,only occasionally in a restaurant,on the street - he was always very friendly towards me.

4. No, I never to my knowledge used any of the 'Karno' bits or routines in/ our films,but Charlie,took bits from several of them also adapted two or three of the shows bodily - one was

Stan Laurel

849 OCEAN AVENUE
SANTA MONICA, CALIF. 90403.

MR HANK JONES,

7245, FRANKLIN AVENUE,

LOS ANGELES. 46. CALIF.

(APT. 22.)

BURY GOLDWATER.!

ENVELOPE FROM STAN LAUREL:
NOTE HIS SLY COMMENTARY ON THE REPUBLICAN PRESIDENTIAL CANDIDATE AT THE TIME

A LOS ANGELES TIMES CARTOON
THAT RAN AFTER STAN LAUREL PASSED AWAY

ASCAP MEMORIES

As I mentioned, every summer, while on summer break from our colleges (Stanford and San Jose State), Dean Kay and I along with our pal Larry Ray (Hayes) would make the rounds of the Hollywood music publishers, trying to get our songs placed to eventually be recorded. The three of us had been writing songs together since our high school days and were amassing a growing catalogue of tunes. Dean and I had hoped to get on a label as artists ourselves, but, in the event that couldn't be accomplished, having a song recorded by a major act was also a goal. Hy Kantor of Robbins, Feist, and Miller Music and Paul Mills of Mills Music, both veteran major players on the music scene, were especially interested in our tunes and very supportive of our early efforts. We in turn enjoyed being around them, relishing their remembrances of the music business back when it was "Tin Pan Alley." Larry was really instrumental to our musical growth as he diligently and tirelessly made the Hollywood rounds of publishers and A&R men touting our songs, trying hard to get them placed.

How we hustled! I remember as a young songwriter the three of us driving all the way up to Harrah's Club in Lake Tahoe. We wanted to pitch a song we had written especially for the nightclub act of the legendary "Last of the Red Hot Mammas," Sophie Tucker. When we finally arrived at her hotel, we called her room. A male voice gruffly answered the phone and said, "Hello." I replied, "Good afternoon, sir. I'd like to speak to Miss Tucker please." The voice answered curtly, "This *is* Miss Tucker! WHOOPS!

In our constant efforts to explore the music scene, one time we were put in contact with a little old lady named Grace Long who had been writing songs just for her own pleasure for many years. She had heard we were writers also and wanted to meet us. We arrived at her cozy home in the Bay Area, and there she was at her piano - looking for all the world like Mary See on a candy box. In a quavering voice, she offered us tea and cookies, and then asked if she might play one of her songs for us. And so she started ... "I love to sit on my veranda - and rock, and rock, and rock..." Her sincerity, wholesomeness, and just plain goodness overwhelmed us. It was all we could do to keep from blubbering in response to being so touched by the sincerity of her music.

Dean, Larry, and I finally were elected to membership in the American Society of Composers, Authors, & Publishers in the early 60s. Joining this prestigious group had long been an ambition of ours. The eminent music scholar Deems Taylor and Stanley Adams, ASCAP's President, signed our certificates of election. Larry was fortunate to have the sublime lyricist Johnny Mercer, whom he met at a bar one night when the master was feeling no pain, nominate him for membership.

My first ASCAP meeting at the Beverly Hilton Hotel in 1963 was a thrill. The Society's semi-official greeter at the door was an old songwriter named Wolfie Gilbert. We chatted for awhile, and he was very interested in what we had written and if we'd had any success yet. I knew his name was familiar, so I asked Wolfie what songs he had composed. He responded with an answer that made my jaw drop: "Oh I just wrote a little number called, "Waitin' For The Robert E. Lee." I realized that I was in the presence of history.

It was such fun to mingle with some of the greats of yesteryear. Rudolph Friml, a tall and elegant man who had written classic operettas in the 20s like "Rose Marie" and "The Vagabond King," was there holding court. Jimmy McHugh, his head as bald as a billiard ball looking spiffy in a checkered coat with an ascot, made the rounds; he was the composer of "I'm In The Mood For Love," "On The Sunny Side Of The Street," and "I Can't Give You Anything But Love." Ned Washington, a dapper man with a tiny pencil-thin moustache, worked the room; he had written wonderful oldies like "When You Wish Upon A Star," "The Nearness Of You," and "I Don't Stand A Ghost Of A Chance With You." Harry Ruby darted about swapping stories with his compatriots and touting horses running at the track; he was the subject of the MGM film biography "Three Little Words" and had composed "Who's Sorry Now" and songs for many of the Marx Brothers pictures. I remember one gathering when Harry Richman, a huge star in the 1920s from George White's Scandals and the Ziegfeld Follies, sat forlornly on a hard backed chair. He was all alone waiting for someone to remember him. It was so sad, as he was a huge star in his day as a singer (he introduced "The Birth Of The Blues") and songwriter too ("Walking My Baby Back Home").

Sammy Cahn and Jimmy Van Heusen, Sinatra's favorite songsmiths whom we first met when we all did a tribute to them on the "Tennessee Ernie Ford Show," were a loud and very vocal presence at the meetings. Van Heusen, known as "Chester" to the Rat Pack, was a notorious procurer of willing women - such an infamous rouè that that aspect of his life almost overshadowed his musical talent. Cahn was frenetic type and frustrated performer himself, always on call to write his trademarked special material lyrics for Friar's Roasts and other inside events. {Ironically, as Sammy Cahn lay dying in his home, his last words were "Dean Kay!" Dean was serving on the ASCAP Board of Directors with Sammy at the time.}

The irrepressible George Jessel often attended. He was something else! His shiny toupee was shellacked down over his forehead, and he always wore a military uniform of suspicious design bedecked with medals that made him look like an officer in search of his regiment. His foghorn voice echoed through the room like chalk on a blackboard. Jessel was one of the true survivors of the vaudeville era, starting out at the age of nine with Gus Edward's schoolhouse act and then capping it all by headlining innumerable times at the Palace (singing his trademarked song, "My Mother's Eyes"). It was he who named Frances Gumm, "Judy Garland." Jessel was known for his moving eulogies at show-business funerals. It was said that he often did three eulogies in one day; at one service, fatigued from his long day at so many memorials, Jessel supposedly looked down at the coffin of the deceased and surprisingly exclaimed, "My God - I KNOW this man!" In his later years, he loved dating women who were young enough to be his granddaughters, even unfortunately when he became somewhat senile and doddering. One of his last flings was with a good actress-friend of mine with whom I did a public television series, "You In Public Service" in the 70s. She told me that one night, after a long night of partying and clubbing, they were in bed together. Jessel started calling her "Natalie," confusing her with one of the famous Talmadge sisters of the silent screen era with whom he had an affair with in the 1920s. That did it. My friend gave up men for good and became a confirmed lesbian.

Probably my most memorable ASCAP meeting was the year the Society gave Fred Astaire a very special award for his contributions to American popular music. The press corps was salivating at the door, waiting to get a glimpse of the retired icon in one of his few public appearances. The door finally opened and out strolled a rather frail elderly gentleman wearing a bright orange-colored hairpiece. He seemed to stagger from the barrage of flashbulbs popping wildly around him as the photographers descended and practically enveloped him. He somehow reached the stage and got to the microphone, no thanks to the rude paparazzi who kept hiding his view with their cameras and blocking his path. Showing the class he demonstrated in his seventy years in the public eye, he held up his hands and asked for quiet. Mr. Astaire then firmly but politely asked all the photographers milling around in front of him to please SIT DOWN, "so that I can see and thank the songwriters of America - to whom I am so very much indebted - for making this day and my career possible." CLASS!

Ira Gershwin became a recluse after his brother George died so young in 1937 and never ventured out to attend any ASCAP functions. However, as I had always been fascinated with all-things-Gershwin, we exchanged letters over several years. He was very kind in answering my questions and went out of his way to straighten out just which songs from "Porgy And Bess" he did *not* write which were attributed to him wrongly in certain Gershwin biographies. On my piano here at home is a personally inscribed photo of Ira that he sent me some years back - needless-to-say, one of my true treasures.

I certainly never reached the league of all these ASCAP greats, but I kept plugging along writing songs alone after Dean and I split up as a recording and performing team. With demos arranged by Butch Parker and Don Ralke, I made the rounds of publishers in between my acting gigs. My old friend Billy Strange, who produced Nancy Sinatra's "These Boots Were Made For Walkin,'" took my song, "I'll Stand On My Own;" Good Ole Boy Joe Bob Barnhill published quite a few for his company. My song "Boots" was published by bandleader Les Brown's brother Warren at MCA Music. It was about a dog that was run over by a car and had the immortal lyric line, "And then as if to say 'so long,' he raised his paw - and Boots was gone." That kept me out of the big-time for years.

But our old pal Hy Cantor at Robbins, Feist, and Miller was the one who really kept encouraging me the most to keep writing. His door was always open, and Hy generously gave me helpful tips to improve my craft. He used to call me, "The Young

Cole Porter," which certainly was a vast exaggeration but a much-appreciated boost to my confidence. It was Hy who spotted the potential of a song I had written as a country tune for Roger Miller called "Midnight Swinger." The moment he heard it, he immediately called his friend Dave Cavanaugh across the street in the Capitol tower and asked him to give it a listen. Dave, who had produced some of Frank Sinatra's, Peggy Lee's, and Nat Cole's biggest hits, thought it would make a great big-band-sounding number for his Capitol artist Mel Tormè. Mel recorded it on his "A Time For Us" album and performed it in his act; his version of the song when he sang it on the Hugh Hefner "Playboy After Dark Show" still pops up on cable TV every so often. Happily, some in the music industry seemed to like the song, and it was placed on the ballot in the initial Grammy nominations the year of its release. And now with the emphasis on "lounge music" of the 60s and 70s, it's getting more radio airplay around the world today than it did when Mel was still alive. Just last week for instance, I got an ASCAP "Midnight Swinger" royalty check for its being played on the radio in Singapore, Sweden, and Ireland! Who'd a thunk??

Our buddy Larry Ray went on to great success in the marketing end of the music business. He went to work for record distributors Bob Chatton and Sid Talmadge in the Bay Area and then LA to learn the ropes and then went into record promotion for several major labels such as Kapp, Electra, and A&M. After starting out plugging such "easy-listening" artists as Liberace and Jack Jones, Larry was very instrumental in furthering the careers of such mega-hit rock and folk artists as Judy Collins, "The Eagles," and "The Doors." For a few years he ran his own label, "Tumbleweed Records," based in Colorado. He now resides on beautiful Whitbey Island in Washington with his lovely wife Marlyne where he writes books, designs websites, and enjoys the good life. He has never forgiven me for getting the lead in our San Leandro High School production of "Kiss Me Kate," because he felt he deserved it more. What Larry fails to appreciate is that I looked much better wearing my four pairs of tights than he ever would.

But of the three of us (Kay-Ray-Jones), it was Dean who soared into the musical stratosphere. He wrote the huge hit, "That's Life." The way that song got off the ground is a book in itself. Dean initially took it to publisher Kelly Gordon, who worked in the lower echelons at Four Star Music. He liked the potential of the tune very much, but Kelly said it needed work and added just a few words to the lyrics. A publisher's job is often to help edit a song to make it more marketable; but, probably due to Dean's being somewhat "green" in the industry, Kelly got his name on the tune as co-writer, just for some very minor changes in a couple of lyric lines. Dean eventually realized he'd been "had" and later bought back all the future writing royalties that would have gone to Gordon from Kelly's estate.

O. C. Smith had the first record of the song, and then Frank Sinatra recorded it - and the rest is history. Actually, Dean did not like Frank's changes to the lyric at the end of the song ("I'm gonna' roll up in a big ball and die - MY, MY."), making it pretty much a downer - much different than Dean's more positive original concept. So Dean insisted that on all published versions of the sheet music, the song had to be printed as he wrote it initially.

The "MY, MY" ending to the tune is a story in itself also. Sinatra always controlled his recording sessions with an iron fist and ran a tight ship. Jimmy Bowen, the producer on the date, was new to him, but had the balls to ask Frank to make another take of the song after he thought the first few were too tame. He wanted more "fire" in Sinatra's delivery. Well, he got it. Sinatra was so pissed off at Bowen having the nerve to ask him to do it again that he spit out the final version of "That's Life" with undisguised hostility at his young A&R man. The "MY, MY" ending was pure anger on Sinatra's part directed right at Jimmy Bowen listening in the booth. But it worked, and Sinatra's version of the song will go down in recording history as a true classic.

As "That's Life" rose on the charts, Sinatra flew Dean to Las Vegas and introduced him from the audience there. Talk about a thrill! When Frank finally passed away a few years ago, along with "My Way," "That's Life" was often played around the world on tributes and news programs as part of the Sinatra musical eulogy. The royalties flowed in again for Dean when Sinatra died. About six months after his passing, Dean called me up and said, "Gee - I sure wish Frank would die again." He needn't have worried: Bono and U-2 recorded it last year. Dean has continued to be an active force in ASCAP, and it's a tribute to his talent and musical knowledge that he's been elected to it's Board Of Directors eight times now. I'm *very* proud of my old partner and friend.

Dean had a really strange experience in regard to "That's Life" and Sinatra's passing that would have made a nice addition to one of my two *Psychic Roots* books. On May 15, 1998, he wrote me :

"Hank:

> 'Frank Sinatra was pronounced dead at 10:50 p.m. in the emergency room of Cedars-Sinai Medical Center, said his publicist, Susan Reynolds,' according to the bulletin issued by the Associated Press

> Last evening, for some reason, I was compelled to download an MP2 clip of Sinatra's version of "That's Life" and save it to my desktop. I'd never done that before ... in fact, I never knew HOW to do it before. The news of Sinatra's passing started breaking here on the Coast at about 1 - 1:30AM.

> This morning, I took a look at the properties of the Sinatra clip icon. I had downloaded it at 10:50PM.

Dean"

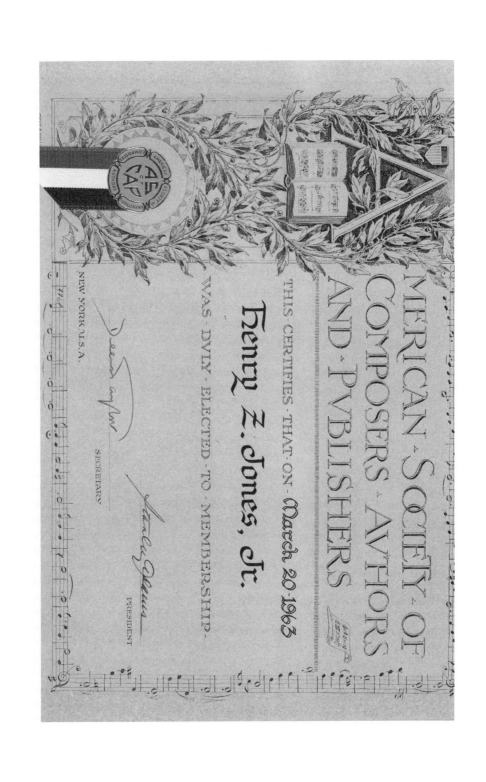

AMERICAN·SOCIETY·OF
COMPOSERS·AUTHORS·
AND·PUBLISHERS·

THIS·CERTIFIES·THAT·ON· March 20 1963

Henry Z. Jones, Jr.

WAS·DULY·ELECTED·TO·MEMBERSHIP·

NEW YORK U.S.A.

SECRETARY

PRESIDENT

WISHIN' WELL

Words and Music by LARRY RAY, DEAN KAY and HANK JONES

Recorded by **HANK** and **DEAN** on RCA Victor Records

WHEN PERFORMING THIS COMPOSITION PLEASE GIVE ALL PROGRAM CREDITS TO

MILLER MUSIC CORPORATION
1540 BROADWAY • NEW YORK 36, N. Y.

PRICE **60¢** IN U.S.A.

HANK & DEAN WITH THEIR CO-SONGWRITER & FRIEND, LARRY RAY

For "Hank" Jones —
With all best
Ira Gershwin

IRA GERSHWIN
1021 NORTH ROXBURY DRIVE
BEVERLY HILLS, CALIFORNIA 90210

November 3, 1970

Mr. Hank Jones
4444 Simpson Avenue
North Hollywood, California   91607

Dear Hank Jones,

      Sorry about the delay but I finally got
around to getting and enclosing a photograph for you.

      And thank you for your kind sentiments
about the Gershwins.

      You say you've read practically everything
available about our work. Well, David Ewen's new and
amplified biography, George <u>Gershwin, His Journey to
Greatness</u>, is just out. Generally it is a sprightlier
account than his 1956 book.

      By the way, do you know my book <u>Lyrics on
Several Occasions</u>? It was published by Knopf in 1959
and I believe it is still in print. Should you get hold
of a copy I'm sure you will find it of interest.

      Good luck to you.

            Sincerely,

            Ira Gershwin

            IRA GERSHWIN

Monday

Dear Hank Jones,

Should you get hold of Ewen's new biography of G. G.: I have written to Mr. E. about Index VII. in which I am credited with 5 songs I had nothing to do with. Mr. E. assures me the proper attributions will be given in the next edition. It was pretty careless to give me credit for "Summertime," "A Woman Is a Sometime

Thing," "Nobody But you," "Do It Again," and "Somebody Loves Me."

Whoever compiled Index VII should have known better as the rightful lyricists of these numbers are correctly named in Mr. Ewen's own book, American Popular Songs published by Random House a couple of years ago.

Too bad.

Ira Gershwin

MIDNIGHT SWINGER

Words and Music by HANK JONES

●

Recorded by MEL TORME on CAPITOL Records

Leo Feist inc.

NEW YORK N.Y.

85c

Tormé Today:

Now on Capitol, and singing better than ever.

MY THREE SONS

Yes, in 1963, Dean was drafted and we left the Ford Show. Although I had taken ROTC at Stanford, I couldn't serve in the military because, after taking the physical, my weight was said to be too light compared with my height. In hindsight, this was a blessing, because most all my fellow-Stanford-ROTCers who did continue on in the army ended up being 2nd Lieutenants in Viet Nam. Many didn't come back.

Our manager George Burke had to figure out what to do with one half of a singing team. Some of Ernie Ford's associates had contacts with the prestigious William Morris Agency in Beverly Hills, as did George. As I had participated in some comedy sketches on the Ford Show, they tuned in on some of my remaining shows to see what I could do and then expressed an interest in me. After meeting with Elliott Wax, their Vice President, I signed a contract for representation with the Morris office and,son of a gun, I was an actor!

The very first audition I had, lucky me, landed me a job. I went over to Desilu/Paramount studios with Elliott to meet with Edmund Hartman, writer of many Abbott & Costello, Jerry Lewis, and Bob Hope pictures and now producer of "My Three Sons." Just before going up to his offices, we ran into movie star (and later TV's "Father Knows Best" and "Marcus Welby") Robert Young, also a client of the Morris office. Elliott introduced me to him by saying, "Hank, of course you know Robert ..." I interrupted quickly by fawning, "Oh, I'd know Mr. TAYLOR anywhere!" Mr. Young gave one of his patented chuckles and ignored me for the rest of the conversation. What a beginning!

Ed Hartmann welcomed me graciously, and we chatted about my experiences with Ernie and the gang. I read a few scenes from the "Three Sons" script, passed muster, and was hired on the spot. "My Three Sons" had already been on the air a few years and starred Fred MacMurray. Mr. M. owned part of the show with Don Fedderson and part of his deal was that he wouldn't have to work hard. His contract guaranteed that he would film all his scenes for the entire year's episodes within two or maybe three months and then go home. Any scene any of the other actors had with Fred MacMurray was usually filmed with the script girl, Adele Sliff, saying Mr. M's lines to us to which we then would react. By carefully splicing the scenes together with skillful editing, it appeared that Mr. M. was actually there in the scene with us, but most often he was not - just carefully inserted in post-production editing. What a gig for him. To paraphrase Mel Brooks, "It's good to be 'da star!"

The "My Three Sons" set was on the Desilu lot. I often would see the world's most famous redhead on lunch breaks. Lucy owned the studio, and she knew it! I'd often have to jump out of her way as she careened around the lot driving her golf cart, her fabled red hair up in pin curls, swearing at me and everybody else in her path to "Get the f --- out of the way!" (Some thirty years later at The National Genealogical Society Conference in Valley Forge, Pennsylvania, where I gave the banquet speech, I ran into her daughter Lucy Arnaz. We talked a while, and I said "I have lots of memories of your mother on the Desilu lot." Without missing a beat, she asked me, "You mean in the golf cart?")."

The soundstage where we filmed "My Three Sons" had wonderful, old musty smell to it. It had been built in the 1920s and absolutely reeked of Hollywood history. There was an excitement to the whole process of making that show that's hard to put in words. You'd sit around for what seemed like forever waiting for the set to be lit by the Director of Photography. After everything was set and looking good, the DP would finally growl, "OK boys, we've got it." Then a loud bell would sound and someone would yell, "Quiet! We're rolling!" Then another voice would say, "Speed!," and we'd be off and running.

I played "Robbie's" friend "Pete" on the program every so often. Robbie (Don Grady) was the middle son on the show and graduated to being the oldest son when Tim Considine left the series. Even though I was a Stanford graduate and 22 years old in 1962 when I started the show, because I looked so young I played Don's *high school* buddy (in a few later color episodes, we eventually went off to college together). Don's mother Mary Grady was a prominent children's agent in town and did a fine job raising her son. Quiet Don was thoughtful, generous, and kind - a pleasure to work with (he later went on to follow his real love and composed music for many television programs, including the "Phil Donahue Show" theme). I really didn't have much to do with Stanley and Barry Livingston who played "Chip" and Ernie," as they were much younger and usually were off to school on the studio lot in between takes. (I ran into Barry in Universal City about ten years ago, still small and wearing thick glasses like he did on the show, but now almost totally bald).

We had fun. I remember that we had a scene in a malt shop once. Somebody had to say "Pass the catsup ..." We had to stop filming until they checked with the sponsor (Heinz) to see how to pronounce that word ("ketchup" or "catsup"). Such was the power of the sponsor that the world stopped for at least a half hour (and big expense) until the clarification came thru. I forget which way was the correct one - at least there weren't 57 choices.

Another wacky memory: we had a scene in a schoolroom on one of the episodes. Just before the camera rolled, the assistant director noted that the blackboard was empty, with no writing on it. So he asked one of the extras to hurriedly go up and just write some gibberish on the board to make it look like a real schoolroom blackboard. She did. We started filming a few takes until there was this big yell from behind the camera. On the blackboard, the extra had written "What was the Mann Act?"(the law that promised punishment for anyone taking a girl over a state line for immoral purposes). We had to film everything again from the top, with muttered curses from the a.d., but smiles and winks from the cast and crew.

The real treat for me on the early black and white "My Three Sons" was working with a genuine show business legend, William Frawley, the curmudgeonly "Uncle Bub" on the program. Bill was superlative character actor and a real character himself. After years of playing supporting roles in films such as "Going My Way," "Miracle On 34th Street," and "The Adventures of Huckleberry Finn", he hit his stride as the irrepressible Fred Mertz to Vivian Vance's Ethel on "I Love Lucy." Their hostile real-life relationship was legendary. Del, the script girl on "My Three Sons" who befriended me early on, was also script supervisor on the old "Lucy" program. She told me that Bill and Vivian wouldn't speak to each other at all when the cameras weren't rolling, so vehement was their mutual anger towards one another. Del would have to be the go-between: Bill would say, "Del, would you please tell Miss Vance to move two steps to the left - her fat ass is blocking my key light;" to which

Viv would reply,"Del, would you tell that old fart hambone to go shove it." On and on ...

It was said that Bill Frawley drank a little (and more). I never saw that, but he moved feebly and had to be sort of carefully led around the set when he was called. But the old boy still had an active libido and great affection for the opposite sex. No young starlet's backside was safe from a Frawley pinch when she wasn't looking; in today's world, it might be considered sexual harassment, but no malice was intended. I had quite a few scenes with Bill in an episode called "The Chaperone" and found that, in spite of his infirmities, he would gather his strength and growl out his lines like he did fifty years before. I fondly remember that whenever he arrived for the day's filming, you could tell the great affection and respect the cast and crew held for him.

When he got too old to work, Bill Frawley was succeeded in the "Uncle part" by William Demarest, a veteran of many Preston Sturges films that are classics today. Demarest scowled a lot and was kind of a grump. I once inquired about the health of his friend Spencer Tracy (with whom I once nearly collided on the MGM lot when Tracy was wobbling along on his bicycle, and neither of us was looking where he was going). Taciturn Demarest wasn't about to share his feelings with any young novice actor like me, so it was a pretty brief conversation and ended before it began.

Although I had had several "My Three Sons" that had scenes with Fred MacMurray that were spliced together in editing to make it look like we really were filmed together, I finally had a chance to work with the star in person in an episode called "The Teenagers." I remember Mr. M. being very quiet and reserved and smoking his pipe a lot. It was a fun script: Robbie and his pals were being chastised for raising money for charity by having someone go topless in a parade float. Well, the topless student turned out to be ME in a oversize bathing suit! For years I never could get hold of that particular show on tape until I finally received a DVD copy last year thanks to the kindness of an Australian fan of the show, Geoff Brown, who generously sent me that "lost" episode.

Boy did my boney knees and hairless sunken chest look great in that bathing suit!

FRED MACMURRAY, DON GRADY, & HANK JONES
"MY THREE SONS" - 1963 (SMUDGED POLAROID TEST)

PRODUCER: ED HARTMANN	GREGG-DON PRODUCTIONS	EXEC. PROD: DON FEDDERSON
DIRECTOR: GENE REYNOLDS	CALL SHEET	ASSOC. PROD: FRED HENRY
ASS'T DIR: SID SIDMAN	"MY THREE SONS" 5272-30	PRODUCTION: JOHN STEPHENS
LOC: GOWER - STAGE 11	DATE: WED. 12/18/63	SHOOTING CALL: 8A

SETS	SCENES	D/N	PAGES	CAST NOS.
EXT. DEBBIE'S PORCH (# 156 BLS)	35	N	2 2/8	5-248-249
INT. HIGH SCHOOL CORRIDOR (GYM)				
(#156 BLS)	36 thru 46	N	3 1/8	5-238-240-241-245-248-249-250-251-251A-X
INT. HIGH SCHOOL CORRIDOR (LOCKERS)				
(#156 BLS)	32	D	6/8	5-248-X
INT. HIGH SCHOOL CORRIDOR (LOCKERS)				
(#156 BLS)	20 thru 22	D	5 2/8	5-238-240-241-242?-243?-245-246-247-X

NO.		CHARACTER	MAKEUP	READY ON SET
2	WILLIAM FRAWLEY	BUB		N/C
3	STANLEY LIVINGSTON	CHIP	9A School	
4	TIM CONSIDINE	MIKE		N/C
5	DON GRADY	ROBBIE	7:30A	8A
6	TRAMP	DOG		N/C
7	BARRY LIVINGSTON	ERNIE	9A School	
8	MEREDITH MAC RAE	SALLY		N/C
238	PAT MORROW	LISSA	8:30A	9:30A
240	BOBBY DIAMOND	MARK	9:15A	9:45A
241	HANK JONES	DON	9:15A	9:45A
242	JOHN PERROW	STAN	9:15A	9:45A
243	KEVIN O'NEAL	JACK	9:15A	9:45A
245	LINDA FOSTER	AMBER	8:30A	9:30A
246	DOREEN TRACY	MARGARET	10A	11A
247	DEBORAH HUNT	CHRIS	10A	11A
248	ANN JILLIANN *	DEBBIE (M)	7:30A	
249	BARBARA WAITE	ARLENE	7A	8A
250	HEATHER MENZIES *	MONA (M)	9A	
251	JANICE KAHN *	LUCY (M)	9A	
251A	NINDY MASTERS *	GRETCHEN (M)	9A	

* DO OWN HAIR BEFORE ARRIVING AT STUDIO

ATMOSPHERE:	SPECIAL PROPS-LIVESTOCK-RIGS & PIC CARS
3 Standins - 7A	
8 Boys & 8 Girls - 10A	

CREW CALL:

1 Cameraman 7:30A 1 Op. 7:30A	1 Script Sup. 7:42A 1 Dia. Coach 7:42A
1 Asst. Cameraman 7:12A	1 Sound Mixer 7:42A
1 Gaffer 7:30A 1 Best Boy 7:30A	1 Mike Man 7:30A 1 Recorder 7:30A
5 Elec. Ops. 7:30A	1 Cable Man 7:30A
4 Grips 7:30A	P.A. Oper
Green Man	Spec. Effects Man
2 Prop Men 7:30A	Standby Painter
2 Makeup Men 7A	1 Craft Service 6:30A
1 Hairdresser 7A	1 Teacher 9A & 1 @ 7:30A
1 Lead Man W/N	1 First Aid ON LOT 7A
1 Swing Man W/N	Stillman
1 Costumer Men 7A	1 Costumer Woman 7:12A

MISC. & TRANS.- GOWER STAGE 11	THURS. 12/19/63-STAGE 11
2 Hardtop Portable Dr. Rms.	EXT. HIGH SCHOOL & STEPS (#156 BLS)
Mkup & Hairdress tables as is	INT. LOCKER ROOM CORRIDOR (#156 BLS)
Lit & Ready 6:48A	INT. LOCKER ROOM (#156 BLS)

MY THREE SONS CALL SHEET - 1963

HORRAY FOR HOLLYWOOD

This probably would be a good place to say something about "Tinseltown." Hollywood is not just a dream, it's also a place. It was founded at the end of the 19th century by a Kansas couple, Daeida and Harvey Wilcox, who purchased 160 acres there for their orchard of fig and apricot trees. The Wilcoxes were devout Methodists and, hard as it is to believe today, envisioned Hollywood as a dry community free from alcohol. In 1887, Harvey Wilcox divided his land into a grid of avenues and streets, and a peaceful affluent neighborhood gradually emerged. The community flourished as purely a residential area until the first movie company arrived to take advantage of the lovely locale and the sunny weather in 1911. In 1913, Cecil B. DeMille, Samuel Goldfish (later "Goldwyn"), and Jesse L. Lasky formed their Feature Play Company and shot their western movie "The Squaw Man" in an old barn in Hollywood - and the town was off and running ...

Mel Brooks says that "Hollywood is like two Newarks." I faintly recall my very first visit to Hollywood in the late 50s when Dean's Dad, Al Thompson, took us there. We stayed at the Hollywood Knickerbocker Hotel on Ivar Street. Once a thing of beauty, like Hollywood it had faded somewhat to a somewhat shabby reminder of the past. We were thrilled to see our "first" Hollywood celebrity in the lobby there: Peter Potter, emcee of "Juke Box Jury;" how we wished then he would play one of our record demos - he didn't. It was at the Knickerbocker in one of its rooms that Ralph Edwards surprised Stan Laurel & Oliver Hardy on his old "This Is Your Life" program. Stan, who insisted on rehearsing everything to perfection, absolutely hated being on that show and almost didn't go through with the rest of the program after they sprung the surprise.

On our summer sojourns to Hollywood while still at college from 1959 thru 1961, Dean and I stayed with Dave and Doris Pilkington in La Cañada. It was an easy drive from there over the hills down into Lotus Land. The record companies we wanted to see were all over the geographical map. Some like RCA, Liberty, Columbia, and Dot were within the two mile square area of Vine Street on the west to La Brea on the east, and Hollywood Blvd. to the north and Sunset Blvd. on the south. Others were further out towards the Strip and Beverly

Hills such as Reprise; but we made the rounds and got to know the territory.

After leaving the Ford Show in San Francisco in 1963, I commuted back and forth between San Leandro and the Los Angeles area for several months. I usually stayed at an inexpensive motel called the Sunset Lodge on Sunset Blvd. in Hollywood. On a piece of stationary from that motel, I wrote the following on November 25, 1963:

"I am writing this in Los Angeles, alone at a motel, watching the funeral of President Kennedy on television. I drove down here to begin my first acting job since leaving "The Ernie Ford Show" in July. It was to start today ("My Three Sons," starring Fred MacMurray), but was postponed due to our day of National Mourning. I will miss Thanksgiving in San Leandro with my wife's family, but it is a small price to pay considering the grief of the nation.

I first heard the news in the kitchen of my home while sorting index cards on "The Irish Palatines." I was listening to the FM radio when a nervous announcer broke in saying, "Here is a bulletin from the KFOG newsroom: "The President of the United States and Gov. John Connolly of Texas have been assassinated while riding in an open car in Dallas, Texas." I sat stunned for a few seconds. Then I phoned my mother at home (who hadn't heard), my father and my wife (who had), and, for some inexplicable reason, my manager in Hollywood. I then turned in on the television, which seemed to be entirely devoted to the event. My friend and partner Larry Ray phoned and told me that the President had died (I had talked to him earlier, and he had heard the news when his wife called).

Then Chet Huntley read an unconfirmed report that Pres. Kennedy had died. I not only didn't believe it, but as I came more and more to "accept" the news, it just didn't "sink in." It still hasn't three days later.

Then the next morning or I guess it was on Sunday - my Dad woke me up and called on the phone and said: "They shot Oswald." I said, "They shot him?!" and Deanna thought I was talking about Lyndon Johnson. Quickly I turned on the set and heard the terrible addition to our tragedy.

I had seen President Kennedy and President Johnson in Washington, D.C. in 1957. My father and I went to the Senate where both men were Senators. I wrote down in a notebook I was carrying that "Senator Kennedy was a leading figure and shows promise as a leader." Johnson was the Majority Leader of the Senate (That was the same trip we sat a few seats behind the Eisenhowers at the Young Republican's Convention).

I would have voted for Mr. Kennedy in 1964, although my leanings have always been Republican in nature. He was a <u>man</u> more than eclipsing a <u>party</u>. His youth and own mispronounced "viga" was attractive to a young person such as myself. I have appeared on ABC-TV network with Mr. and Mrs. Robert Kennedy on "The Ernie Ford Show" in 1962, and Mr. Kennedy made some kind remarks about my work and talent. Since that first-hand contact with that remarkable family, I had grown more-than-interested in their beliefs. Although differing from my beliefs in economics, their (his) foreign policy was identical with my own: <u>liberality with reason</u>.

Perhaps the death of this great son of America - indeed a martyr already - will somehow shake America enough - as a nation and as individuals - to proceed with better and firmer thoughts of our own good fortune and duty. We must not allow one thing for which he stood die or be forgotten. Then, he would truly be dead. We must, instead, use his memory as a living legacy of what we should do and what we should be!

I plan to do my part to sustain his living spirit.

May his death be only a physical thing -

Hank Jones
November 25, 1963"

In reading this over again forty-plus years later, I don't quite know what I meant by "liberality with reason," but at least I was sincere in trying to put down what I was feeling in that terrible time.

After his six-month stint in the army was completed, in 1964, Dean and I moved into an apartment together in Hollywood at 7245 Franklin Avenue. It was managed by an old lady and her 300-pound son named "John." The landlady was nice, but the son was sinister. I often found myself alone in the creaky elevator with him riding slowly up to my floor. It seemed as if we'd never get there. He had that wild-eyed gaze that made me feel like he was hiding an axe behind his back. He didn't, but it sure was spooky. The building was populated by an assortment of Hollywood types: agents, studio secretaries, acting wanna'-bes, and an occasional lady of the evening (and afternoon and morning too, depending on her clientele). Dean liked to practice his guitar during the afternoon hours, and his chord changes would sometimes be interrupted by a sharp knock at the door from the lady in stiletto heels and skimpy bikini next door who told him in no uncertain terms that his loud playing was hurting her matinée business. My friend Marv Sachse, who lived there too, made a bet with the same young woman who didn't believe that he really would dive from his top-floor apartment balcony into the swimming pool far below. He did the deed, and won the wager - but I don't know if and how he collected.

Fast, longtime friends emerged from those Franklin Avenue days. Arlene Briggs from Marblehead, Massachusetts and Karen Miller from Texas moved in downstairs and immediately became pals. Diane Tietz resided across the way in the next apartment building with her roommate Elaine Thompson, and Dean and I got to know them both well. Diane helped me pass the long hours waiting for the phone to ring with innumerable games of Scrabble and lots of delicious home-cooked meals and chat. Diane, a former beauty queen who at one time was married to a man named "Tietz," loved to give me a bad time by leaving word with my answering service lady saying, "Just tell him that Miss Tits called." Oh well, it was Hollywood - they probably had heard it all at the service and didn't think a thing about it. Now "Diane Beach," she lives in Las Vegas today and still is one of my best friends.

It was a lonely time when I first arrived. I was looking for a young-adult church group to attend to help me find new friends. Someone told me that Roy Rogers and Dale Evans had helped organize just such an organization for young people in the entertainment industry, so I decided to go check it out.

The initial meeting took place at the old Hollywood Knickerbocker Hotel which I have mentioned before, that musty relic of the past that had seen better days and was now well past its prime. Our group met in an interior room of that ancient building that was chock-full of people when I arrived. I felt rather claustrophobic, I remember, because the room wasn't air-conditioned and had no windows for ventilation. The heavy drapes hanging from the four walls made the site seem even more oppressive. I must say, when they closed all the doors, I wanted to leave.

I'm glad I didn't. The guest of honor that night was Elmer Bernstein, the famous film composer. Bernstein was wonderful! He spent his part of the program regaling us all with marvelous stories about his life in music and demonstrated some of his compositions on an old grand piano in the room. At the climax to his talk, he announced that he "would now play a piece he wrote for the score of Cecil B. DeMille's classic movie *The Ten Commandments*." It was the beautifully majestic theme that was used whenever God was spoken of in the film.

The *very* moment his hands touched the piano keyboard something amazing happened. That closed room came alive! A whoosh of air from nowhere rushed through the entire facility, as the heavy drapes against the walls billowed forth and flapped wildly. This intense burst of energy continued on for a good fifteen or twenty seconds. And just as suddenly as it started, it stopped. In an instant, it was over.

There was a silence from the crowd that you could cut with a knife. And then, someone in the back row chuckled. Soon the room was filled was cascades of laughter as we all began to appreciate what had transpired. "God's Theme" indeed!

I continued going to the Hollywood Life meetings and figured eventually it finally was time to become a member. It was supposed to be an open group made up of anyone who had grown up attending a Christian church of some kind in their hometown, which I did. So I talked to the leaders of the group about officially joining. "Of course you can," said the President, Bob Turnbull, "but in order for us to include you you must sign this lists of 'beliefs' saying you completely agree and accept them." Well, I *didn't* agree with many of those fundamentalist doctrines they presented and told them so. And they in turn told me then that I couldn't be a member of Hollywood Life. So I walked.

I was back to "Square One." As my folks were life-long Methodists, I started attending the Hollywood First Methodist Church, a gigantic building on the corner of Franklin and Highland Avenues not too far from my apartment building. It was a good choice. They had a lively preacher in Rev. Charles Kendall, a thriving congregation, and - best of all - a choir and pipe organ that blew the roof off the church when they made music. Over the years, it became a second home on Sunday mornings and many good friends were made there. Later on, my then-wife Lori carved a special niche there as the wedding director and went on to well-deserved success at neighboring Wilshire Methodist Church also. One of her most memorable weddings at Hollywood was when she engineered the wedding of one of the singing "Temptations:" the bride and groom "vogued" down the aisle after being pronounced man and wife, doing their groovy Motown moves all the way to the front door of the church.

Eventually, I became an usher, along Jeff Wilhelm whose children attended school with Amanda. The church attracted an interesting mix of Hollywood folk: actors like James Shigeta of "Flower Drum Song," Jan Hooks from "Saturday Night Live," and Sonny Schroyer from "Dukes of Hazzard" all attended, along with former Secretary of State Warren Christopher and new age writer Marianne Williamson (who was, as they say in today's lingo, extremely "hot"). Jeff and I had to be sensitive to some of the unique souls who dropped by, because they certainly were following their own drummer. For instance, there was our regular attendee "Michael" who often interrupted the sermon by running down the aisle saying, "I gotta' pee," as well as the woman who insisted on showing her devotion by walking up to the altar and raising her dress above her shoulders in spiritual celebration before someone gently took her aside. The church has served the Hollywood community well now for many years, and today essentially has a preponderance of gay members who feel right at home there, as well they should. My buddy Jeff Wilhelm, formerly a film and TV writer, felt "the calling" and did a career turn-around in his fifties. He went back to school, graduated from seminary, and has just been ordained an Episcopal priest. I think that's terrific!

The streets of Hollywood were safer in the 60s when I arrived. It really was still a predominantly residential community, but with its own kind of off-the-wall twist. There was a sort of official greeter who walked the avenues glad-handing tourists with a great big "Howdy." I never knew his name, but he dressed up in leather-fringed western garb with a big cowboy hat and had a beard and moustache like Buffalo Bill - so that's what we always called him. You'd never know just who you'd see on any given day. I remember running into Percy Kilbride, "Pa Kettle" of the Universal movie series, dressed in a dapper English tweed suit with a derby, tipping his hat to the ladies on Vine Street. I'd often see character actor Donald Crisp, who had started in silent films and was in such classics as "Lassie Come Home," at Safeway in the meat section of the store picking over the steaks. Gabby Hayes - *yes*, Gabby Hayes - would get out of his spiffy sports car and stroll around town in a classy gray suit, his beard nearly covering the ascot around his neck. When I would visit Sy Devore's Barber Shop, in the next chair I'd hear a distinctive voice, and it often would be either Jim Jordan who was "Fibber McGee" on radio or punch-drunk prize fighter-actor Slapsie Maxsie Rosenbloom. Of course there were the panhandlers and touts and the bookies and tarts also who made up the varied citizenry, and the mix was always fun and exciting. My favorite was the memorable black guy who drove around Hollywood in a white Cadillac convertible with seashells glued all over it. It had a big gold sign painted on its side that said "I Love White Women!" He got a lot of attention.

One of my old Bay Area pals whose friendship continued once I arrived in town in the 60s was "American Top 40" disc jockey Casey Kasem. Casey came to LA about the same time I did and immediately rose to the top in his field with his magnificent microphone skills and knack for spotting rising musical talent. He would be in the back row at Hollywood First Methodist Church most every Sunday, and afterwards we'd often go out to dinner and just chat about our dreams. In spite of his great success as a DJ, Casey's real goal was to become a major actor. He was actually very good and did the best Peter Falk "Columbo" imitation I've ever seen. One night we went together to hear Bishop James Pike from San Francisco speak on his experiences trying to contact his dead son from the afterlife. It was an intriguing talk, and I know it helped steer me into the area of paranormal research that eventually resulted in my two *Psychic Roots* books. The one thing I should have learned about Casey (but didn't) was *never* to play Monopoly with him, which we often did at his home in Laurel Canyon. Talk about cutthroat: he was tough and showed no mercy. He always won. On the Top 40 of Monopoly players against Casey Kasem - I was number 1,245 - without a bullet.

AH, THE MOVIES

In July 1, 1964 I recorded an entry in my "Day At A Glance Book:"

> "Made my first movie today at MGM's Stage 30 in Joe Pasternak's 'Girl Happy.' A small role, but it was thrilling and certainly a start. Also in picture are Shelley Fabares, Gary Crosby, Chris Noel, and that fine character actor Harold Stone, with whom I did a scene. Met Elvis Presley - very nice fellow. Gave him 'hello' from Ernie Ford, and he thanked me. Director was Boris Sagal."

It took a long way to get there. I had been up for a much larger role in the same picture and almost got it; but eventually was told that I was too young-looking for the part (an excuse I would hear over and over again when up for other potential jobs throughout the 60s and 70s). It was disappointing because I had lots of callbacks and came very close. Dean, Larry and I also came super-close to getting seven songs we wrote into the picture for Elvis to sing. In the acting audition process, I had received advance copies of the script for "Girl Happy" and showed it to my song-writing buddies. On "spec," we wrote a bunch of tunes that we thought would be right for the film. I must say, even hearing them today forty-plus years later, they were indeed GOOD songs. We met with Freddy Bienstock, Elvis's publisher, at his suite in the Beverly Hilton and played them for him. He liked them very much and promised to play them for Joe Pasternak, the producer of the film, and Colonel Tom Parker, Elvis's manager. A few weeks later, Bienstock told us he could indeed get them in the movie - IF we would put Elvis Presley's name on all those songs as co-writer of each number and give his company total publishing royalties. We balked, thinking this was unfair and even immoral as Elvis didn't write those songs, WE did. So, our big chance to get seven songs in a Presley picture fizzled when we stood our ground. I don't want to even imagine the potential royalties over the years that we lost by making that principled decision. Years later, songwriter Hal Blair, who wrote many Presley hits like "I Was The One," told Dean that that was the way Presley's music publishing *always* worked: no Elvis as co-writer and publisher on the song - no deal.

My first impression of the King Of Rock and Roll after arriving on the soundstage at MGM was totally against type: there he was in a high-backed director's chair, smoking a stylish cheroot, and reading the <u>Wall Street Journal</u>. As I passed on Ernie's personal regards to Elvis, I remember shaking his hand and thinking that he had the softest hand I'd ever felt in my life. It was weird. But it was such an important day for me because I finally was meeting the person whose music had made such a dent in my psyche and impelled me to pursue my own musical dreams.

As I later wrote in my book *Psychic Roots; Serendipity & Intuition in Genealogy*:

"Presley couldn't have been nicer to me. He was every inch the southern gentleman and a pleasure to work with. Elvis was truly in his prime then and seemed to have the whole world at his command. So it was especially sad to see his gradual disintegration from the effects of prescription drugs and the pressures of super-stardom in the years that followed. When he passed away, I was devastated and felt a sense of personal loss.

When CBS-TV broadcast his last filmed concert performance on October 3, 1977, I almost couldn't bring myself to watch it. The evening the special was aired was traumatic for me. I was so emotionally distraught and grieved at the loss and waste of such a good man, the tears were flowing even before the program began. As I sat back in my chair, stressed out but determined somehow to watch Elvis's final appearance, I felt an unknown energy, almost an electricity, pulsing throughout my living room. It was so strong I could almost touch it. Then at the very mini-second the show began, a large, framed picture of my daughter hanging on the wall opposite my chair crashed to the floor with a gigantic boom. In all my years of living in that house, no picture had ever fallen and none ever did again.

I've thought and thought about that incident
many times since then, its exact and precise
timing as the concert started, my state of mind at
that moment, and especially the profound sense
of grief I was feeling. To most others, it would
have been just a picture falling off the wall, an
occurrence of no real import. To my mind, then
and now however, it was a true synchronicity - a
coincidence involving internal and external events
that had a very special meaning only to me.

For the rest of the entire evening I had the
eerie feeling that an unseen presence was with
me during that concert. It was uncanny and
downright spooky. I can't help remembering that
at the end of every Presley public appearance, an
announcer would always get on the p.a. system
and close the show by announcing, "Elvis has left
the building." In my home the night of October 3,
1977, I wasn't so sure that he had!"

In 1965, I began work on my second film, "Village Of
The Giants," a reworking of H. G. Wells "Food Of The Gods." It
was directed by Bert I. Gordon, and the cast included Beau
Bridges, Johnny Crawford, Tommy Kirk, Toni Basil, Tim Rooney,
and Ronnie Howard. It was a terrible script and one review said
"even the special effects are bad." But hey - it was exposure
and it was money. We filmed it at Paramount and at the
Columbia Ranch in the Valley. In one climactic scene, Jim Begg
and I had to lower Johnny Crawford by rope down in between a
model of starlet Joy Harmon's giant bazooms (made twelve feet
tall by the prop department). The utter lack of taste of this
scene was not surprising, as my very first line in the film was
when two groups of teens - boys *and* girls - are in a knockdown,
drag-out fight and end up in a big heap of flailing bodies. From
the bottom of the pile, I pull out a large bra and utter the now
immortal words, "Hey, who's a size 40?" It was downhill from
there.

I remember taking my Dad, who was visiting LA on
business, to the first screening of "Village Of The Giants" on the
Paramount lot. I don't know who squirmed the most at the
appalling final product that we saw on the screen: him or me. It
figures this movie was even once voted one of the "50 Worst

Films Of All-time." I'm so proud! Ever after, whenever I would run into Beau Bridges at Disney or some other studio, we would pass each other with a wink and a slight smile - knowing we had a common secret in that SOMEHOW we both had survived this classic turkey.

I made two good friends during production of "Village Of The Giants:" Johnny Crawford and Jim Begg. Johnny was a true teen idol when he made the film, having starred with Chuck Connors in the long-running TV western "The Rifleman" and also having several top-40 record hits on DEL-FI. Johnny was somewhat shy and so cautious about who he would let into his life. I remember he kept changing his phone number all the time to ensure that no teenybopper would invade his privacy. He was quite a film buff, and we spent many happy evenings at his beautiful home in the Hollywood hills looking at classic movies from his 16mm movie collection. Today Johnny dresses up in black tie and tails and fronts a very successful dance-band orchestra specializing in jazz and pop music from the 20s and 30s.

Jim Begg and I played buddies in the movie. Jim was a smart cookie. He was one of the few actors I knew who invested his money wisely and felt comfortable in the business part of "show-biz." I had come to LA from the Bay Area alone except for Dean, and Jim kindly included me in his circle of young friends - kindred spirits all hoping to make it big in a town that kept trying to keep you small. Jim introduced me to talented folks who today, forty years later, are close pals like Jerry Rannow, Jewel Jaffe, Marty Ross, Bernadette Withers, and Eddie Applegate. We've all become supportive and nurturing friends thru thick and thin. When I had my major cancer surgery recently, along with Dean, Larry, Lou Wagner, Jan Williams, Pete Renoudet, Jeff Wilhelm, Mimi Weber, Gloria Burke, and so many others, they all rallied around me as if no time had passed at all. I love them dearly for it.

In 1966, I was cast as "Loren Fairchild" in the Universal Studios production of legendary screenwriter Richard Mattheson's "Young Warriors." It was a big part that required lots of preparation. We had two weeks essentially going through basic training - a movie boot camp - so that we looked like we really knew how to march and handle a gun. The Pentagon sent us a Colonel who was a technical advisor to make sure it all looked real. We even had to eat K-rations to feel the experience of what these young World War II soldiers went through: yuck - pork and egg yoke was nauseating. I played the stereotypical green recruit, the son of a funeral director who was always talking about how his father went about embalming, "re-hanging the ears," etc. Being so green and vulnerable, it was inevitable that I would be killed by the NAZI bastards at the end of the picture. To make it as gory as possible, the Germans not only shot me in my foxhole, they bayoneted me in the stomach too as I futilely screamed for my buddies to help me ("HACKER!! HELP ME, *PLEASE!!*") My parents came to the preview of the film and had to look away when I kicked the bucket: now THAT'S acting!

The picture starred TV's "The Virginian" James Drury and featured mostly all Universal contract players except me and Norman Fell. They were paid practically nickels and dimes because of their lousy contracts, but Norman and I at least got some pretty good bread because we were freelancers and not bound to the studio's cheapness. Jim Drury was pleasant, but a little surly too. We almost lost a couple days shooting when, on a weekend away from the set, he got into a barroom fight and the other guy pulled out some of his hair. The rest of us all bonded, as good soldiers should, and several of the group have remained friends. Robert "Buzz" Pine was in my platoon. He went on to co-star on TV's "Chips" series and later his daughter Katie went to school with my daughter Amanda. I shared a foxhole with Jonathan Daly also, and we became fast friends. He too had started on a variety show (with George Gobel) and went on to much success as a writer/director with his own theater company as well as an actor (being co-star of "The Jimmy Stewart Show" and of acid-tongued Don Rickles' "CPO Sharkey"). Jonathan now lives in Hawaii, and we still love to banter about old-time character actors like Franklin Pangborn, Burt Mustin, and Minerva Pious, hoping that someday perhaps later generations will be bantering about us too.

Jonathan wrote an additional scene for the film for himself, Tom Nolan, and me where we chased a duck through a minefield. It was silly, but gave the picture some much-needed humor. Tom, a prominent kid actor in his younger days, eventually became one of the best writers on the scene, with pieces often in *LA Magazine, Playboy, Rolling Stone, The LA Times,* and *The Wall Street Journal.* He's penned books about mystery writers Ross MacDonald and his wife Margaret Millar and is currently working on a biography of Artie Shaw. Like Jonathan, Tom and I still stay in touch, and, when we get together, share old war stories. The duck, unfortunately, did not survive to participate in our World War II veteran's reunions at Musso & Frank's Grill (unless we ate him there by mistake).

We shot "Young Warriors" at Universal Studios. The head honcho there was a silver-manned, well-manicured slick dude named Lew Wasserman. He'd been a former agent at MCA and ended up running Universal with an iron fist. It was said he had some behind-the-scenes help from "Da' Boys" in making things run smoothly with the unions there. I remember seeing Mr. W. at the Universal commissary often while we were shooting our war epic. One lunchtime, he was heading for the commissary door when a young brash underling jumped ahead of Mr. Wasserman. He just wanted to hold the door open for him and earn some brownie points. Unfortunately, in order to get to the door quickly, the guy had to elbow and jostle some female secretaries who were heading for the same destination. As this junior Sammy Glick was fawning over his boss and trying to make an impression on him - no matter how he did it, Mr. Wasserman glared at the young man, pointed his finger right under his nose, and said firmly and simply, "WRONG!" The point was made, and the junior executive looked like he wanted to fade into the woodwork.

I remember that working at Universal Studios was different than working anywhere else in town. The brass there was worried that our filming might interfere with the smooth flow of the Universal City Tour buses that were everywhere on the lot, not the reverse as one would expect. The sad truth was that the tours often made more money for the studio than the movies did - thus the priority. The bosses at the studio almost had apoplexy the day that craggy-faced character actor Neville Brand, one of the most decorated soldiers in World War II, got roaring drunk one afternoon, came out of the sound stage on which he was shooting a TV show, and promptly peed on the tour bus and its occupants as they drove by. He was barred from the lot for life.

Not content to have the Germans kill me in "The Young Warriors," I allowed the Japanese equal time to shoot me down in the Oscar-winning 20th Century Fox epic "Tora-Tora-Tora." I played "Davey," a young civilian pilot trainee who happened to be taking his first flying lesson over Pearl Harbor on that day that will live in infamy, December 7th, 1941. Most of the cast got to go on location to Hawaii to film, but I was stuck on a soundstage in Culver City in front of a rear projection screen. I have really nice billing in the movie, but my part was whittled down an awful lot from the length it was originally. What happened was that the studio gave the Japanese unit almost carte blanche to film their side of the attack, and when they screened the first rough cut of the movie supposedly their portion was over seven hours long - and that didn't even count all the film the American unit had shot. So chop-chop, snip-snip, there goes Hank. I will say though that that scene is well-remembered by fans of the film who see it on its frequent reruns on TV. It's hard to forget my vulnerable bright-yellow tiny Piper Cub as it's surrounded by the entire Japanese armada of fighter planes readying to attack Pearl Harbor, with accompanying dialogue between Jeff Donnell and me that also will live in infamy, *"I better take over, Davey!" "Ok, Miss Fort!"*

DAILY VARIETY DAILY

Thurs., July 16, 1964

MGM 'Girl' For Jones

Hank Jones, singer regular on ABC-TV "Tennessee Ernie Show" past 18 months, has been cast in MGM's Elvis Presley-starrer, "Girl Happy," thence to "Special Date" episode of "My Three Sons."

Wed., Mar. 16, 1966

Jones Joins 'Warriors'

Hank Jones, former comic on ABC-TV's "Tennessee Ernie Ford Show," was signed yesterday by Universal producer Gordon Kay for role of an Army private in "The Beardless Warriors," s t a r r i n g James Drury, Steve Carlson, Jonathan Daly and Robert Pine.

Wed., Nov. 16, 1966

Film Castings

Hank Jones, "Blackbeard's Ghost," Disney.

THE Hollywood REPORTER

Hank Jones Has 'Affair'

Hank Jones guest stars in "A Waltz From Vienna" seg of "Family Affair." Charles Barton is directing script by Hannibal Coons and Charles Marion.

Wednesday, May 22, 1968

SOON—AT YOUR FAVORITE MOTION PICTURE THEATRE

"VILLAGE OF THE GIANTS"
Will never be the same because of

HANK JONES   JIM BEGG

CR. 4-7541
Rep.:
Burke & Weems Assoc.
280 So. Beverly Dr.
Beverly Hills, Calif.

Rep.:
Kal Ross
8440 Sunset Blvd.
Hollywood, Calif.
OL. 4-2200

PRODUCTION CALL SHEET

PROD. No. 20036   TITLE   VILLAGE OF THE GIANTS - COLOR STD   DIRECTOR   BERT GORDON

SHOOTING DATE   TUESDAY,   MAY 11,   19 65   W.A.   7 4 3 7

MADEUP AND READY TO SHOOT AT 10:00 A.M. - STAGE 5

SET#	SET	SCENES	CAST	D/N	PAGES
2	INT. BARRY HOUSE	29-30 PT	1-2-3	D	2 1/2
2	INT. BARRY HOUSE	57-58X-59PT-62-63X	1-2-3	D	1
2	INT. BARRY HOUSE	173-175	1-2-3-4-13	N	1 1/4
2	INT. BARRY HOUSE	316-316A	1-2	D	1/2
2	INT. HOUSE	334	1-2-4-13	D	1/2
	LATER - STAGE 14				
3	INT. BASEMENT (GENIUS ROOM)	141-145-147 1H 150-142	6-7	N	1 1/2
3	INT. GENIUS ROOM	381-382	1-3-4-13-17 18	N	4

CAST	ACTOR	CHARACTER	MAKEUP CALL	SET CALL
1	TOM KIRK	MIKE	9:30 A.M.	10:00 A.M.
2	CHARLA DOHERTY	NANCY	9:00 A.M.	10:00 A.M.
3	RON HOWARD	GENIUS	9:00 A.M.	10:00 A.M.
4	JOHN CRAWFORD	HORSEY	W/C	
6	TIM ROONEY	PETE	W/C	
7	BOB RANDOM	RICK	W/C	
13	TONY BASIL	RED	W/C	
17	JIM BEGG	FATSO	W/C	
18	HANK JONES	CHUCK	W/C	

WELFARE WORKER
STANDINS AS ORDERED

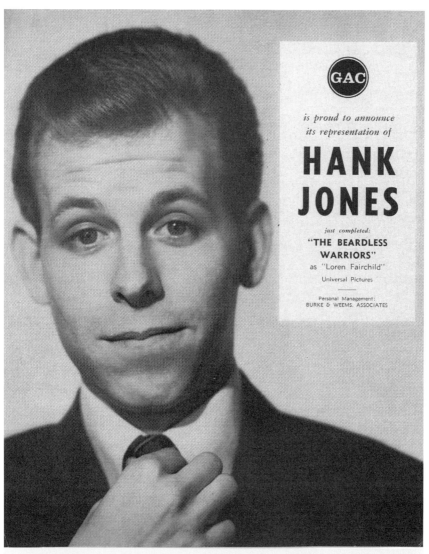

"VARIETY" AD FOR UNIVERSAL'S "YOUNG WARRIORS"

STEVE CARLSON & HANK JONES IN
UNIVERSAL'S "YOUNG WARRIORS"

DIRECTOR JOHN PEYSER (LEANING BEHIND CAMERA)
CALLS "ACTION" TO HANK JONES IN UNIVERSAL'S "YOUNG WARRIORS"

JAMES DRURY & HANK JONES IN UNIVERSAL'S "YOUNG WARRIORS"

HANK JONES AS "LOREN FAIRCHILD"
IN UNIVERSAL'S "YOUNG WARRIORS"

BUYING THE FARM IN "YOUNG WARRIORS"
WHAT A DEATH SCENE!

Hank Jones Wins Tora! Roadshow Role

Hank Jones has been set by director Richard Fleischer for featured role in "TORA! TORA! TORA!" roadshow for 20th Century-Fox.

Jones, former Disney contractee, plays young airman having a flying lesson over Pearl Harbor when Dec. 7 Japanese attack commences.

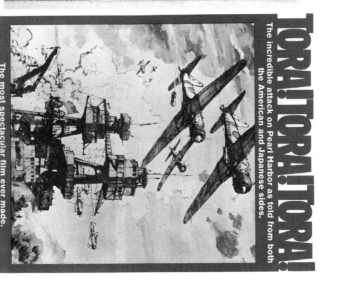

TORA! TORA! TORA!

The incredible attack on Pearl Harbor as told from both the American and Japanese sides.

The most spectacular film ever made.

53rd DAY OF SHOOTING

TWENTIETH CENTURY-FOX FILM CORPORATION

SHOOTING CALL *9AM*

CALL SHEET

DATE *Mon. May 12, 1969*

PICT. *TORA, TORA, TORA*   NO. *A888*   DIR. *R. FLEISCHER*

SET		SCS.	LOC.
SET		SCS.	LOC.
SET *EXT. CORNELIA FORT'S STEARMAN*		SCS. *126, 127A, 274,*	LOC. *STAGE 5*
SET *PLANE. (PROCESS) (D) 1⅝ PGS.*		SCS. *358, 360, 362, 364*	LOC.
SET		SCS.	LOC.
SET		SCS.	LOC.
SET		SCS.	LOC.
SET		SCS.	LOC.

CAST AND DAY PLAYERS	PART OF	MAKEUP	SET CALL	REMARKS
JEFF DONNELL (NEW)	CORNELIA FORT	8 AM	9 AM	RPT. STAGE 5
HANK JONES (NEW)	DAVEY	8:30 AM	9 AM	X
MAKO (NEW)	YOSHIKAWA	8:30 AM	9 AM	

ATMOSPHERE AND STANDINS		THRU GATE		
STANDINS		8 AM		RPT. STAGE

TUE. 5-13-69 - STAGE 5
INT. LANDON'S B.17
   PROCESS

ABOVE CALLS SUBJECT TO CHANGES

Hank Jones Set for 'Tora!'
Hank Jones has been set by director Richard Fleischer for "Tora! Tora! Tora!" at 20th-Fox.

ASST. DIR. *D. HALL / R. WATT / J. RICKARDS*   UNIT PROD. MGR. *W. ECKHARDT.*

HANK JONES
MOVIE TIME

With
Deidre Hall as
Adam an Eve

In
*"Herbie Rides
Again"*

With
Jeff Donnell in
"Tora-Tora-Tora"

With **Kurt Russell**
in *"The Barefoot
Executive"*

BLACKBEARD'S GHOST

I am so proud to have been thought of as a "Disney Familiar Face" in the 60s and 70s. I mean the Disney artists even drew a cartoon of me! It all started in 1966. One of my agents at General Artists Corporation, Max Arno, heard that the studio was looking for someone to play a major role as the bumbling head of the college track team in their forthcoming production of "Blackbeard's Ghost." It was to star Oscar-winner Peter Ustinov in the title role. Max then sent over a print of my latest movie, Universal's "Young Warriors," for producer Bill Walsh, director Robert Stevenson, and Walt Disney himself to look at. Somehow I passed muster, because within just a few days I got the call from the Disney brass that Hank Jones was now in the movie as "Gudger Larkin."

After working hard at home going over my script, memorizing all my lines, and developing my nebbish character, I arrived at the studio in early December of 1966 to begin filming. What a welcome! The Disney Studio in the 1960s was like summer camp. Everyone smiled, really because everyone was just plain glad to be working there. The boss set the tone of the team atmosphere: he would get angry if someone ever called him "Mr. Disney" instead of "Walt." On my first day, I noticed that the security guard at the gate looked familiar - kind of like a sad-faced basset hound. Later on I realized why I thought I knew him: the Disney animators had used his unique visage as a model for one of the characters in their "Lady And The Tramp" film - and here he was making sure I had a studio pass to get on the lot.

After warm greetings from Bill Walsh and Robert Stevenson, I was ushered to my dressing room adjacent to the huge sound stages. My "roommate" was Michael Conrad, a superb character actor later to achieve fame as Sergeant Phil Esterhaus on TV's "Hill Street Blues." I was in seventh heaven, absolutely delighted and thrilled to be working at Disney. But all Michael seemed to do was kvetch about how he was doomed to be "in some f**king cartoon," as he so crudely put it. I shrugged off his grunts and grumbles, and said I was just happy to be working - anywhere.

After make-up and wardrobe - before I could even say "Bibbety-Bobbety-Boo!" - I found myself under the lights, finding my mark, and ready to begin my first scene with Dean Jones. The first shot we filmed took place at Blackbeard's Inn. The set depicted the massive interior of a rickety old hulk of a building (later enhanced and enlarged by the superior matte work of renowned artist Peter Ellenshaw). The first ten minutes of the picture Dean and I together set up the whole story line to follow: of how as the new athletic coach he comes to Godolphin College to try to bring new life to its failing track team (of whom I am the wimpy Captain), aided mysteriously and magically by the ghost of Blackbeard the pirate (played with over-the-top zest and wonderfully-pure ham by the great Peter Ustinov). In the initial scene at the inn, Dean Jones introduces me to the school's Dean (portrayed in all his curmudgeonly "bald-dom" by Richard Deacon - known to his friends as "Deac," so memorable as put-upon Mel Cooley on the old "Dick Van Dyke Show"). I remember being tense and nervous during the first few takes, actually saying a quick silent prayer that I would remember my lines and not screw up. But as the scene got rolling, I gradually started to relax. Dean and Deac put me at ease, and I felt I was among friends. After my first tight solo close-up, Deac smiled, winked at Dean and said, "Hey - he's *funny*!" I needed that. But my confidence really soared between takes when I went back to my canvas-backed chair while they lit the next shot. Dear Elsa Lanchester sat down right next to me, looked me in the eye, and told me "That was a *very* good scene!" To paraphrase the immortal words of Sally Field, "They liked me - they really liked me!" Ah, actor's security.

We poked along filming. Robert Stevenson directed every shot using story-boards that Disney animation artists drew for him - then painstakingly recreated every sketch drawn with us live actors. It was slow going, sometimes taking forty-five minutes to light a scene which would then yield only ten seconds of film. My Dad and Mom visited the set one day and just couldn't understand the snail's pace of shooting. But the day they showed up just happened to be a day when only "Blackbeard" and I were working. When my folks arrived at the studio and were shepherded onto the soundstage, all they saw amongst the clutter of cables and lights were two snazzy director's chairs sitting side by side: on the back of the first chair was written "Peter Ustinov;" on the back of the second chair right next to it were the words "Hank Jones." I couldn't have set that scene up better if I'd scripted it myself.

Character actress Elsa Lanchester, who played "Emily Stowcroft," was a real piece of work. The former Mrs. Charles Laughton had been in many classic films, including "David Copperfield," "Lassie Come Home," "Witness For The Prosecution," and "Mary Poppins," but was probably best remembered for her shrieking portrayal of "The Bride Of Frankenstein" in that beloved Universal horror sensation. Elsa had her beginnings in the English music halls in the 20s (as did Stan Laurel) and never lost her ribald sense of humor. Her dry asides between takes continually broke all of us up and made it difficult to settle down with a straight face when it came time to shoot our own scenes.

But Elsa's finest hour was on even a grander scale. The Disney artists had spent months painting a huge backdrop the length of the entire soundstage for the big track race sequence near the end of the movie. On the backdrop were literally hundreds of portraits of individuals seated in the grandstand watching the race. "Real" actors and extras were then strategically placed in front of the "fake" ones on the backdrop to make it look like a crowd of thousands were cheering me on to win the big relay. True to Disney quality, each figure on the painted backdrop had a very real and distinctive look to him or her. One day on lunch break, Elsa walked the entire cast down the whole length of the backdrop and made up risqué (all right - downright DIRTY) comments about each painted figure. We laughed so hard at her raunchy descriptions that the tears just streamed down our faces. We all had to go back and have our make-up redone to continue shooting the picture.

I had first met Dean Jones, the lead in our film, a few years earlier at an ABC-TV press party, when we were plugging "The Tennessee Ernie Ford Show," and he was hyping his "Ensign O'Toole" series. By the time we did "Blackbeard's Ghost," Dean was Disney's resident star, appearing in such popular family films as "That Darn Cat," "The Ugly Dachshund," and "The Love Bug." He was easy to work with and followed Jimmy Cagney's sage advice about how to act: "plant your feet firmly, look the other guy in the eye, and tell the truth." All of our scenes together in "Blackbeard" and those we did in succeeding films made me look better thanks to Dean's natural performances and likeability. He did cause us some production delays, however. Dean had a fairly heavy beard that grew very fast, and we would have to wait before every close-up he had so that he could go back to his dressing room and shave before every take. It was worth the wait.

His co-star Suzanne Pleshette was and is one of Hollywood's most genuinely-liked performers. She is beautiful, sexy, super-bright, says it like it is, ... and has the foulest mouth in town. My introduction to Suzanne's somewhat warped sense of humor occurred the very first day of filming. We actors were all seated in a circle just off the busy set when the noon hour arrived. As the assistant director yelled, "One hour everybody," Suzanne seductively eyed all the males in the group and purred, "Well, who wants to hump me for lunch?" I'm sure we all secretly desired to be first in line, but discretion ruled and nobody took the bait. But oh, what might have been ...

I think I've only worked with two real geniuses in my career: Robin Williams (whom I barely survived - more later) and Peter Ustinov. Peter (later dubbed "Sir Peter" in 1990 by Queen Elizabeth II) really thought of himself as a writer as much as an actor; his "Romanoff and Juliet" won awards on Broadway and later made a very successful transition to film. The bearded wonder made his mark early on playing the mad emperor Nero in the epic "Quo Vadis" in 1951. He went on to co-star with Bogie in "We're No Angels" and then brought home an Oscar in 1960 for his thespian efforts in "Spartacus." "Topkapi," "Death On The Nile," "Hot Millions," "Lola Montès," and "The Sundowners" – his film credits bulged with marvelous performances.

How I *loved* being around Peter Ustinov - he was truly one of the most amazing people I've ever known. Fluent in eight languages, he could even speak Greek and Turkish. Lord knows what dialect he would choose to greet you with when you arrived at the Disney lot each day. We sometimes would talk genealogy, and he was most interested that I had started out so early in the field. Peter had quite a background: he was Russian, German, Spanish, Italian, French and - get this - one quarter Ethiopian! His grandfather had been an officer in the Czar's army prior to the revolution. But I think what I really enjoyed about him most of all was his talent as a mimic. He could duplicate the sound of a car engine by year and make of the auto. {"Would you like to hear a 56 MG or a 57?" - and I'll be damned if he could replicate the subtle differences}. But was I ever honored on screen in "Blackbeard's Ghost" when he actually did an imitation of *me*! {"Come on, Coach - we've come in last in two events already!," he whined a la Gudger}.

But one fateful day during filming, it was the heart of Peter Ustinov that made the biggest impression on me. Because of my unusual skinny build and distinctive look at the time, it was difficult for anyone to "double" me. I had a stand-in, Dick Warlock, but he was really too stocky to actually duplicate my meager frame. So during the climactic scenes where I had to run the relay race to save the sacred honor of my Godolphin College, I did all the stunts myself. The trouble was I was running against *real* track stars and, even though I played a puny guy, I had to at least give the illusion that I could win the big race. One of my running competitors Bill Toomey, later famously to win the decathlon in the Olympics for the USA, was designated my coach and masseur. He showed me what to do, how to pace my run, and gave me welcome rubdowns when my legs kept cramping up. Ouch!

One stunt that I had to do as "Gudger" was to fly high up into the air over the stadium as the invisible ghost of Blackbeard propelled me down the track to victory. To do this, I was attached to the fabled "Mary Poppins wires," used so successfully by Julie Andrews in her flying sequences for that wonderful Disney musical (also produced by Bill Walsh and directed by Robert Stevenson). Nearly invisible piano wires came down from a moving dolly on a track high up in the flys of the soundstage and were then attached to a leather harness around my waist hidden under my tracksuit. It shouldda' worked. The Disney special effects crew thought it all out, except for one crucial thing: in "Mary Poppins," Julie's wires were cushioned by her bulky Victorian dresses; in "Blackbeard's Ghost," I was wearing a skimpy track suit and had no protection from the sharp wires cutting into my bare shoulders and arms. So consequently the more I flew, the more I bled. The red stuff was running down my arms trickling right into Ustinov's face below me. His red pirate costume was getting more crimson by the take.

And then it happened - something that supposedly had never occurred before in Disney history. Those blankety-blank wires unraveled from my harness, sending me crashing ten feet below and landing right on top of poor Peter Ustinov. I could have been killed. But typical of the great man, he didn't gripe, he didn't complain, he didn't yell at me to get the hell off of him. All he cared about was if I was hurt in any way and if he could do anything to ease my obvious pain and discomfort. His only concern was *me* - and I've never forgotten that.

Bill Walsh rushed over and offered to stop shooting the whole picture for the day. But "the show must go on," so I said "No, let's try it again." So we did - ten more times. And if you see that flying sequence in the movie, it looks absolutely amazing. You'd never know the real story of what actually happened. But my main memory of the whole event was not the faulty wires or the precipitous fall: it was the concern and kindness shown by Sir Peter Ustinov towards yours truly.

"Blackbeard's Ghost" had a royal cast of character actors to learn from: besides Elsa, Michael, and Deac, there was Norman "Woo-Woo" Grabowski - who had a face that looked like it was run over by a truck, but was in reality a gentle giant; Ned Glass - so memorable as "Doc" in "West Side Story;" Elliott Reid - whose strong presence graced "Gentlemen Prefer Blondes" and "Inherit The Wind;" Herbie Faye - a staple on the Sergeant Bilko series; slick Joby Baker - who became a noted artist later on; Betty Bronson - who shone as "Peter Pan" in the 20s silent version; Bing Russell - Kurt's Dad and a sweetheart of a guy; and so many other familiar faces like Byron Foulger, Gil Lamb, William Fawcett, Lou Nova, Herb Vigran, and Charlie Brill.

I made lifelong friends on the "Blackbeard" set too. There was Jan Williams, who started in the mailroom and was Ustinov's stand-in. On his first day at work, Jan nervously introduced himself to Peter and told him, "I loved you in 'Guns Of Navarone;' to which Peter gently replied, "That was James Robertson Justice". GULP! Jan ended up a full-fledged producer of some of the later "Herbie" movies and now has found great success selling choice real estate for Del Monte Properties up on the Monterey Peninsula.

I met Lou Wagner then too. He was cast as a member of my track team and became a life-long pal. Lou has had much success starting with leads in "Planet Of The Apes," "Airport," a regular slot on NBC's "Chips" series, on and on, and he's still going strong - now looking like a young Paul Muni. I would occasionally visit Lou on the set of his films, one of which I remember with pleasure being "Airport" at Universal; I recall seeing how nice a guy Dean Martin was to cast and crew alike (Dino called *everybody*, even his own sons and daughters,

"Pally" because he had a hard time remembering names). Lou had the best answering machine song ever, sung by his friend, Vern: "Louie Wagner isn't here, but he'll be awfully glad to call you back dear, if you leave your name and number at the beep toooooooone."

Another buddy was Pete Renoudet who worked in art props at the studio. I loved having lunch with Pete whenever I could, because he knew *everybody* on the lot and shared his friendships. Thru Pete, I met the most fascinating people. I especially loved spending time with several of the legendary animators known as "The Nine Old Men," like Ward Kimball, Ollie Johnston, Woolie Reitherman, and Frank Thomas. They were the ones who created and drew "Snow White," Pinocchio," "Bambi," and "Sleeping Beauty," leaving an unparalleled legacy of joy to children everywhere. Pete constantly honed his own acting chops in theater productions all around LA, and it paid off. He's had a role in almost every Disney live-action movie in the 60s thru the 80s and now is making a mint doing cartoon voice-over work. Good guys all!

But besides all the happy memories, "Blackbeard's Ghost" also is draped in black crepe in my mind. It was Walt Disney's last movie. As I arrived at the studio gate on December 15, 1966, I noticed the guard wiping a tear from his eye. All he said was, "I'm not sure if you're working today - Walt just died." We had heard he had had some health problems, but nothing serious was ever mentioned. In fact, he came to the set of "Blackbeard's Ghost" just to see how things were going a few days earlier. We'd seen him unobtrusively standing with his foot on a ladder in a corner of the soundstage watching the shoot. We were stunned when we heard he had passed away in the hospital just across the street from the studio. Nobody could do any work - the whole studio closed for the day in respect and in mourning. The Enchanted Kingdom had lost its Prince.

But life went on. "Blackbeard's Ghost" had its splashy world premiere at the Pantages Theater in Hollywood on February 8, 1968 as a fundraiser for the Southern California Olympians. Sports-legends Bob Mathias, Parry O'Brien, my masseur and coach Bill Toomey, and the great Jesse Owens all were in attendance to give the film a mighty send-off. The premiere drew lots of celebrity guests too, including James Garner, Edward G. Robinson, and Pat O'Brien - all enjoying a troop of pom-pom girls dancing to a live 60-piece band in front of the theater. My parents flew down from San Leandro to attend. I'll never forget my Dad, I guess bursting with pride, going up to Glenn Ford, pointing to me, and bragging to him, "That's my son. He's in the picture!" Ford muttered a somewhat embarrassed "that's nice," and quickly walked away.

The reviews were very good. *Variety* called it:

"A lively and entertaining Walt Disney production which features Peter Ustinov in a tour de farce title role as the restless spirit of the famed pirate. The Buena Vista release has 'the Disney touch,' artistically and commercially with very good box office prospects. All thesps register quite well, including Hank Jones as a goofy track star."

Hollywood Reporter noted:

"At last report, neither producer-writer Bill Walsh nor director Robert Stevenson had spawned cults, nor is it likely they need one. It is the cultists who are missing a good and sure bet. Together and in combination, Stevenson and Walsh combine creative production, unerring direction, good scripts and casts with the work of Hollywood's finest technicians, perpetuating the best tradition of typically American film comedy and qualitative family entertainment, all for Walt Disney and Buena Vista release. The consistency of their record at the box office and in terms of reliable performance is not surpassed, 'Blackbeard's Ghost,' their newest Disney collaboration starring Peter Ustinov, Dean Jones, and Suzanne Pleshette, is one of their best, one for the record book of top grosses, and by the shrewdness of its casting, potentially appealing to an ever broader cross-section of the audience .... The Disney stock company contributes top support including Elsa Lanchester, Richard Deacon, and Elliott Reid. Hank Jones as the young captain of the team is specially bright."

I did quite a bit of promotion for "Blackbeard's Ghost." There was a lot to sell besides the film, including a book and a record album based on it. The Disney artists even made a cartoon character of me as "Gudger" - that was fun. *Variety* noted on April 16, 1968 that "Hank Jones was in town from the Frisco thumping of "Blackbeard's Ghost." I remember that p.r. event as I was heralded as "Prince Charming" (what a stretch!) as I judged a girls aged 10 - 13 "Can You Fit Cinderella's Shoe Contest?" at Fisherman's Wharf. I did some TV shows also plugging my role too, like Woody Woodbury's talk-fest where I appeared with "December Bride's" Spring Byington. Buena Vista, Disney's film distributor, also sent me out to some theaters showing "Blackbeard." They would run the film, and then I would come out from behind the screen to say "hi" to the audience afterwards, explaining how some of the special flying effects in the track sequence were done.

Some forty years later, I still am proud of my part in making this Disney classic. It still holds up. Bonnie and I were enjoying dinner at the Hotel Del Coronado a few years ago with my "Blackbeard" compatriot Lou Wagner and his wife Debbie. As we left the dining room, a woman ran up to me and started spouting the lines that I said as my character Gudger Larkin in "Blackbeard's Ghost." I told her, "Hell, I didn't know those lines when I was delivering them!" She said it was her favorite Disney film of all time - and her kids' too.

Amazing that after all these years ...

PETER USTINOV AS "BLACKBEARD'S GHOST" HELPS HANK JONES AS "GUDGER LARKIN" WIN THE BIG RACE

HANK JONES AS "GUDGER LARKIN" IN
WALT DISNEY'S "BLACKBEARD'S GHOST"

*COACH DEAN JONES GIVES A LOCKER-ROOM PEP TALK
TO HANK JONES IN "BLACKBEARD'S GHOST"*

RICHARD DEACON GIVES A HARD TIME TO
DEAN JONES & HANK JONES IN "BLACKBEARD'S GHOST"

WALT DISNEY PRODUCTIONS

SHOOTING CALL

PICTURE "BLACKBEARD'S GHOST"   NO. 3261   DIRECTOR ROBERT STEVENSON

SHOOTING CALL   9A   DATE THURS. DEC. 15, 1966

STAGE #4

EXT SOUTH BLEACHERS - STANDS

DEAN'S GROUP: SCS PARTS 357-367-367A-367B-367C-426-436-438-443-453-477-479-506-523-605-606.COMP.

SILKY & GROUP WATCH MEET: SCS 392-395-398-452-454-465-478-480-483-505-522-547.

"   "   @ TICKET BOOTH

SCS 368-369-370-372-372A-373-374-THRU380- 380A-381-382-382A-382B-383-384-386-585-604-609 PARTS.

CAST	CHARACTER		1ST CALL	ON SET
X PETER USTINOV	BLACKBEARD		WN	
X DEAN JONES	STEVE WALKER	(2ND UNIT)	WN	
X SUZANNE PLESHETTE	JO ANNE		730A	845A
X RICHARD DEACON	DEAN WHEATON		745A	845A
X MICHAEL CONRAD	PINETOP PURVIS		745A	845A
X HANK JONES	GUDGER	(2ND UNIT)	WN	
X JOBY BAKER	SILKY		WN	
X NORMAN GRABOWSKI	FIRST HOOD		WN	
X LOU NOVA	SECOND HOOD		WN	
X TED MARKLAND	THIRD HOOD		WN	
X CHARLIE BRILL	FOURTH HOOD		WN	

DAY PLAYERS:		
NEW RICHARD COLLIER	TICKET TAKER	WN

ATMOS. STANDINS.ETC.		
X JAN WILLIAMS	SI UTILITY	8A
X LYNN GRATE	SI JONES & UTILITY	8A
X SHIRLEY SMITH	SI JO ANNE & UTILITY	8A
X RICHARD WARLOCK	SI JOBY & UTILITY	8A
X	15 SPECTATORS (STUDENTS)	830A

ADVANCE SCHEDULE

FRI. DEC. 16 (39TH DAY):
EXT SOUTH BLEACHERS @ TICKET BOOTH
            (COMPLETION)

STAGE #4
SCS 368-369-370-372-372A-373-374 THRU380-380A-381-382-382A-382B-383-384-386-585-604-609 PARTS.

MON. DEC. 17 (40TH DAY):
EXT SOUTH BLEACHERS - POM POM

STAGE #4
SCS 409-429-432-433-435-437-441-475-499-501-503-622.

TUES. DEC. 18 & WED. DEC 19-
(41ST & 42ND DAYS):
EXT SOUTHWEST CURVE

STAGE #4
SCS 415-417-419-421-423-424-528-530-534-546-559-574-593-599-608-611-618-350-466PART.

WALT DISNEY DIED TODAY
DIDN'T FILM THIS — STUDIO CLOSED.

SILENT SCREEN STAR OF "PETER PAN" BETTY BRONSON
WELCOMES HANK JONES & DEAN JONES TO "BLACKBEARD'S INN"

"THE STAR OF THE GODOLPHIN COLLEGE SHOTPUT SQUAD"

Friday, February 9, 1968

THE *Hollywood* REPORTER

HANK JONES

Is GUDGER LARKIN

In Walt Disney's "BLACKBEARD'S GHOST"

What's a Gudger Larkin?

THE UNITED STATES OLYMPIANS
SOUTHERN CALIFORNIA CHAPTER
BENEFIT WORLD PREMIERE
WALT DISNEY'S
BLACKBEARD'S GHOST
Pacific's Pantages Theatre
6233 HOLLYWOOD BLVD. at VINE ST.
THURSDAY, FEBRUARY 8, 1968 - 8:30 P.M.
FORMAL

Pacific's Pantages Theatre
WALT DISNEY'S
BLACKBEARD'S GHOST
THURSDAY, FEB. 8, 1968 - 8:30 P.M.
GLOBE TICKET CO. 495

SECTION CNTR
ORCHESTRA
RDW Z
SEAT 102

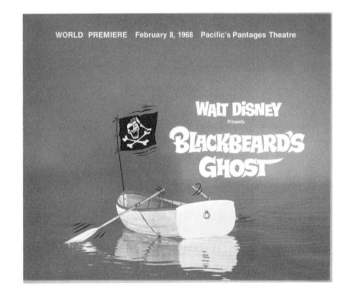

WORLD PREMIERE   February 8, 1968   Pacific's Pantages Theatre

WALT DISNEY
Presents
BLACKBEARD'S GHOST

A Runner-Up in 'Slipper' Contest

1673

By the margin of a slight squeeze, pretty 12 year old Cari Yonemoto of 549-19th Ave., in San Francisco, just missed becoming "Cinderella, but was a runner-up in the "Can You Fit Cinderella's Shoe" contest at San Francisco's famed Wax Museum, last Thursday.

Helping her on with her prize of a new pair of shoes is popular young motion picture and TV star Hank Jones of San Leandro, who is featured in the Disney film "Blackbeard's Ghost" which opened in the Bay area last week. Hank played "Prince Charming" and was master of ceremonies for the occasion.

THE FAMILY BAND
& OTHER DISNEY FILMS

My second film for Disney Studios was one of the last big old-fashioned musicals produced in Hollywood, "The One And Only Genuine Original Family Band." It starred Walter Brennan, Buddy Ebsen, Janet Blair, Lesley Ann Warren, and John Davidson. I'm convinced that one of the reasons they put me in this movie was that I didn't sue the studio after the wires broke as I was flying over the soundstage and fell so hard on Peter Ustinov when filming "Blackbeard's Ghost." Who knows? What I do know is that we worked our tails off making "Family Band" and that it was lots of fun doing it.

The plot concerned the disputed election between Grover Cleveland and Benjamin Harrison in 1888, not exactly the most appealing subject for a movie. The score was written by the prolific Sherman brothers, Richard and Robert, who wrote the words and music for "Mary Poppins" and "The Happiest Millionaire;" those two scoundrels also penned the song that's impossible to get out of your head once you've heard it, "It's A Small World After All." I played the town delivery boy, a Cleveland supporter, who was the nemesis to John Davidson and his Harrison loyalists. The picture was directed by Michael O'Herlihy with whom I'd worked at MGM in 1964.

The studio wanted all the featured actors in "Family Band" to sing and dance in the big musical numbers. So prior to filming, for two weeks Wally Cox, Richard Deacon and I went through basic training as dancers under the personal direction of choreographer Hugh Lambert. I gained great appreciation for the gypsy dance community after that crash course in pain as my poor tired legs and shaky knees will attest. I'm proud to say that when you see the three of us in the film we look damn good, like we actually *belonged* in the dance ensemble with the more-seasoned pros.

I got to know Wally Cox and Richard Deacon well during shooting - we ate lunch together most every day. Wally had gained fame as "Mr. Peepers" in the early days of television. He was indeed mild-mannered and quiet just like his character, but that belied another side of him that wasn't what you'd expect. In his 20s, he was Marlon Brando's roommate when they were both starving actors in New York. You'd think that in their single days between the two of them it would be Brando who would attract all the women: WRONG! Wally was irresistible to the fair sex. He even dated Marilyn Monroe for God's sake!

I remember being with him one day when a zoftig starlet sashayed by. Wally showed his quiet appreciation for her by saying under his breath, "Mmmm - solid comfort!" He was super-bright and, unlike most actors, had no illusions about the trappings of stardom. Once when the crowd surrounding him seemed to be overreacting to his every word and laughing at everything he said, I heard Wally mutter to himself, "Why are they laughing? It's not funny." Wally actually spent much of his off-camera time as a gold and silversmith and used much of his largesse from show business to finance the precious metals he needed for his work. After "Family Band," Wally went on to great success as a regular on the TV game show "Hollywood Squares." This special man died much too young, unfortunately under rather mysterious circumstances. Marlon Brando was so grief-stricken at his friend's passing that he had Wally's ashes placed in an urn on the mantel of the fireplace at his home in Tahiti where they remained until Brando's death.

Big, bald Richard Deacon was like a character out of Dickens. "Deac," as he was called, was jovial and so much fun to be around - a genuinely good guy. His portrayal of slow-burning Mel Cooley, the putupon assistant of Carl Reiner on the old "Dick Van Dyke Show," still breaks me up whenever I see it. Deac worked so hard sweating to master those song and dance numbers in "Family Band" that sometimes I thought he was going to drop dead right there in front of us. It was Deac who introduced me to Dick Van Dyke on the lot and made me feel like I belonged in their company (Dick was also a friend of Stan Laurel, so we had lots to talk about). I would see Deac every so often after "Family Band" was released, and we'd always laugh and make the claim that, between the two of us in that picture, we almost sunk Disney Studios ("Family Band" not being the mega-hit that was expecte).

Walter Brennan was the star of the film, but he certainly didn't act like one. He didn't eat lunch in the special commissary dining room reserved for the "names:" instead each morning his wife made him his midday meal and put it in his lunch-pail, complete with thermos bottle, which he took to the studio almost like he was going to work in a factory. I had worked with Walter earlier on his short-lived TV series "Tycoon." We had some scenes together on that previous show where it was just the two of us in the shot. As we started filming, I could see Walter kind of evaluate me and get a read on what I was doing. He smiled, said "pretty good," then quietly took me aside and started giving me a class in "Film Acting 101." He patiently demonstrated, for instance, how (by looking with my right eye into his left eye) more of my face could be seen by the audience in our scenes together - a little Hollywood trick that, along with his massive talent, garnered him three Academy Awards. All Walter cared about was making *me* look good. I've never forgotten his generosity and kindness, and I was able to use his tricks of the trade on camera for years.

"Family Band" was about two years later, and I could see age creeping up on Walter Brennan. He had bad emphysema by then and was so short of breath that he required an oxygen tank to be hidden by his side as we filmed. On his longer speeches, Walter would say a sentence or two, the camera would keep rolling while he took a hit of oxygen, and then he would continue on with the rest of his lines; the pause for air would then be cut out of the film in editing. But somehow that old trooper pumped himself up and was able to bring forth the dynamic energy needed for the scene each and every time. It was really quite remarkable and a testament to his dedication and fortitude.

Walter was a character actor *and*, I must say, a character. It was never dull. His politics have been described as being "a little to the right of Hitler." Walter's specialty was to wait until the other actors were being made-up, bleary-eyed and out of it at 6 A.M., and then pouncing on them to discuss politics. You couldn't win. All you could do was nod and listen - there was no escape because you were imprisoned in the make-up chair! Oh well, I had literature from the John Birch Society to take home after work. Oh, and he did the *best* Walter Brennan impression I've ever seen!

Buddy Ebsen probably was the most laid-back actor I've ever encountered. In between takes, Buddy would take LONG naps, completely oblivious to all the hubbub going on around him. One time when he was snoring away, the still-photographer got the entire cast and crew - probably one hundred people - to pose around his chair for a group shot and even then he didn't wake up. Buddy had started out as a hoofer in a vaudeville act with his sister Velma. He made lots of movies in the 30s, some with Shirley Temple, and for a while was going to be the Tin Man in "The Wizard of Oz" until he almost died from a bad reaction to the metallic paint on his costume. "Family Band" gave Buddy a chance to dance again. He just glided over the floor with his smooth yet eccentric moves, and I never tired of watching the man in our song and dance scenes together.

The juvenile leads of "Family Band" were John Davidson and Lesley Ann Warren. John and I hit it off immediately. He had a self-depreciating sense of humor and loved making fun of his own leading-man, "guy with the chiseled-chin looks" image. He had a beautiful home at the far end of the San Fernando Valley, complete with horses and butlers. He shared his good fortune with the "Family Band" bunch by inviting us all to have the cast party right there at his house. John's brother passed away during filming, and we all kind of spiritually circled the wagons around him in friendship to help get him through the rough time. Our director, Michael O'Herlihy, wouldn't let John off work to attend his brother's funeral, so the poor guy had to keep going in the midst of his obvious pain. John is still doing musicals today, now playing "grandfather-parts" in "Oklahoma" and "State Fair" in stock productions around the country.

Lesley Ann Warren was young and awfully pretty, just starting to feel her oats in her move from the Broadway stage to Hollywood. She was going then with big-time hairdresser Jon Peters (one of the models for the lead character in the movie "Shampoo") during the shoot, and we all would have lunch on occasion together. I found Peters to be without much of a sense of humor, no sin of course, but still not very easy to talk with at the studio commissary over a "Mickey-Burger." He later went on to run several studios himself and had a long relationship with Barbra Streisand. Lesley Ann really blossomed as an actress later in life (winning an Oscar for her work in "Victor-Victoria") and is still going strong in character roles today.

During the two-week dance rehearsals prior to filming, my eye was caught by one of the girls in the chorus who'd just arrived in Hollywood after appearing as a go-go dancer in Las Vegas. She shone like a diamond among the lesser jewels, with her sexy figure, winning smile, and contagious giggle. She was CUTE in capital letters. Her name was Goldie Jeanne Hawn, and "Family Band" was her first movie. Other guys on the set were attracted to Goldie also, one of whom was a sixteen year old kid who'd starred in several Disney films already. His name was Kurt Russell. Who'd-have believed that all these many years later they'd be a couple, one of Hollywood's most successful, with a great relationship and a bunch of kids to boot. And it all started singing and dancing "West Of The Wide Missouri" together in "The One And Only Genuine Original Family Band."

But of all the people I met filming "Family Band," the one who sticks out in my mind the most was John Craig. He became a lifelong friend. There was only one John Craig, and he was it! He had been born Joe Cline in 1928 in Indianapolis, Indiana. While still a student at George Washington University, he was asked to escort the daughter of the French Ambassador to a reception, as she was 5'11" and nobody else was as tall as John with his 6'4" frame. Having found the expensive French champagne to his liking, in an expansive mood he began entertaining the crowd an impromptu singing concert. Metropolitan Opera star Lily Pons was one of the attendees and was so impressed with John's raw talent that she urged him to try the New York stage and opened some doors there for him. He auditioned for Richard Rodgers (who changed his name from Joe Cline to John Craig) and won the part of Lt. Cable in a national revival tour of "South Pacific." After roles in early TV's "I Remember Mama" and on Broadway with Ethel Merman in "Happy Hunting," he took over the lead role in the musical version of "Li'l Abner" in New York and in Las Vegas. Hollywood called, and John found good roles in many TV series, usually playing the heavy, and some important movies like "Sweet Charity" with Shirley MacLaine (he was "the Big Spender" in "Hey Big Spender") and "Pennies From Heaven" with Steve Martin.

In "Family Band," our director Michael O'Herlihy decided that John, who portrayed one of the townsmen involved in the disputed election, needed a pie in the face during the climatic fight scene; but he wouldn't tell John it was coming and insisted on throwing it himself. Everybody on the set, cast and crew, knew what was going to happen except John Craig. When the cake hit an absolute bulls-eye on John's schnoz and covered him with goop, his close-up reaction was priceless: surprise, anger, and then joy at being the butt of such a wonderful joke.

John is hard to put in words. He LOVED to gossip and tell show business stories. We heard them all. He worked in plays with Joe E. Brown late in his career when the great comic was getting a bit senile. It was John's prime job to steer Joe E. back to the correct script when he often would be saying the lines for one play and somehow jump into the dialogue from a completely different show. And in "Happy Hunting" on Broadway, John was the buffer between musical comedy legend Ethel Merman and her leading man Fernando Lamas. They hated each other's guts. One day the diva less than delicately told John, "If that egotistical Spaniard tries to put his tongue down my throat one more time in our love scenes, I'll bite it off!"

John would tell the same stories though over and over again until everyone knew the punch-lines by heart. He told of how 30s movie diva Miriam Hopkins once was at a party with John where no one was paying much attention to her. Miffed that she wasn't in the limelight, she proceeded to fake a faint and fell to the floor. However when nobody there noticed her swoon, she proceeded to get up, go to a spot where more people were gathered, and promptly fainted again! This time they paid attention.

At one Christmas caroling party we gave in Toluca Lake, we decided to play a prank on John. He began telling one of his old chestnuts that we'd all heard a hundred times before. When he started, we all surrounded him, listening carefully. Gradually one by one as planned, we started moving away and leaving the room. By the time John got to his familiar punch-line, he was totally alone - we'd all left. There was no one to tell the joke to. When he realized what had happened, he collapsed with laughter on the floor, and, of course, it gave him a NEW story to tell.

Lou Wagner traditionally gave a New Year's Day party at his house in Laurel Canyon for all his friends. Lou lived in an old castle-type home that supposedly once had belonged to Liberace. John was invited, as were we all, to the festivities. Unfortunately the first year he was asked to come, John went next door to Lou's neighbor's house by mistake. He said he was there for four hours living it up before he knew he was in the wrong house. The neighbors enjoyed John's stories so much that they invited him to come back the following year.

John was devoted to his mother in what was a strange, almost love-hate relationship. When she finally died, John arranged for American Airlines to ship her body back to

Indianapolis for burial. Unfortunately, Mrs. Craig's coffin got lost somewhere between Los Angeles and Indiana. John was frantic. Finally, after days of searching, she turned up in Texas. The smart-ass counter man at American Airlines, trying to make light of the situation, said to John, "Well I hope she had a good trip." John was so livid at that remark that he sued the airline and won a large settlement. Best of all though, he had a new story to tell about how he lost his mother.

In his later years, John retired to Palm Springs where he remained actively involved in animal-pet charities there. I think only his friend Doris Day had more devotion to the welfare of our furry friends. John's mission was to find every animal a good home, and he often ended up keeping the ones he couldn't place himself. His last dog was a mangy mongrel with absolutely no redeeming qualities - a pet only John could love. This good man continued telling his show business tales about Estelle Winwood, Zasu Pitts, Helen Twelvetrees, and Rex The Wonder Trout to any and all who would listen until his passing from lung and brain cancer in 1999. He is greatly missed.

To honor his memory, here's the joke he told at the party that we all walked out on before John could deliver the punch-line:

"A famous Hollywood producer died. He arrived in Heaven and was greeted by Saint Peter with the news that God was going to make a movie and wanted him to produce it. The producer said he was tired of making movies, and just wanted to enjoy Heaven. But Peter persisted, pointing out that the script was by Shakespeare. The producer hesitated, but declined. Then Peter told him that the music would be by Beethoven. The producer thought it over, but said 'no' again. Peter then said the scenery would be painted by Michelangelo and DaVinci together. The producer finally relented and agreed to make the film. Then Peter told him, 'Now as for casting the female lead, I hope you'll understand …. Er … Uh … You see, God has this girl friend …'"

"Family Band" opened nationwide at the Radio City Music Hall as part of its Easter Show in 1968. The reviews were tepid at best. I think the convoluted subject matter about an election in 1888 that no one really cared about or could identify with was at the core of the poor reception. But, as in so many cases, I have very fond memories of this movie because of all the good friends I made as we filmed it.

I made eight films in total for Walt Disney Studios. After "Blackbeard's Ghost" and "The One & Only Genuine Original Family Band," the next movie I did was "Herbie Rides Again," again produced by Bill Walsh and directed by Robert Stevenson. It starred Helen Hayes and Ken Berry, both of whom I had worked with before. I played "Sir Lancelot," a wimpy drag-race driver who, as would be expected, chickens out at the final moments of the event. The movie was filled with familiar faces from the Disney stock company, and I took special pleasure in noting that the fellow who waved the flag to start my race was Huntz Hall, the elastic-faced comic from all the Dead End Kids films.

After completing that role, I got a call from the studio saying that Walsh and Stevenson wanted me back for yet another part in the same movie. They darkened my skin with full body make-up, gave me new eyebrows and a hippy-dippy brown wig, and son of a gun - I was the surfer dude riding the big waves in Hawaii along with Herbie the Love Bug by my side. I was hidden under so much weird make-up that when I arrived at the soundstage to shoot in front of the blue screen most of my old Disney pals didn't even recognize me. Jan Williams, who had been Ustinov's double and stand-in in "Blackbeard," did a triple take when he finally realized that that gnarly surfer dude was yours truly.

"The Shaggy D.A." was next, again a Walsh and Stevenson vehicle. My old friend Dean Jones starred again and once more Suzanne Pleshette was his leading lady. More Disney regulars were in the cast including Keenan Wynn, Dick Van Patten, Jo Anne Worley, Vic Tayback, Hans Conried, Benny Rubin, and my fellow-soldier from "Young Warriors", Jonathan Daly. I played a frustrated cop trying to corral Dean who had turned into a huge sheepdog - just like real life, right? When I showed up to film a scene with Suzanne, she greeted me with "Where's your track suit?" Once "a Gudger" - always "a Gudger," I guess. A major challenge in this movie was trying not to break up at the antics of Tim Conway, whom I was attempting to arrest in one of the closing scenes. Tim is a bit nuts and his off-the-wall comic riffs make it near impossible to keep a straight face and stick to the script. Somehow I did, but it was tough.

The neat thing about Disney in those days was that once they considered you part of their actors' stock company they'd use you in whatever came along. I was blessed, that's for sure. One morning I got a frantic call at home at 9:00 A.M. from the head of casting asking if I could be at the studio at 10 to be in a picture: the guy they hired didn't show up, and they really were behind the eight ball. So I took the world's fastest shower, put on my grubby jeans, and sped over to the corner of Goofy Lane and Dopey Drive. They slapped some makeup on me, shoved a script in my hand, and the next thing I knew I was spending the day throwing double-takes at an obstinate chimp and doing several scenes with Kurt Russell in "The Barefoot Executive." Other minor roles followed in "Million Dollar Duck," with Dean Jones again, and "No Deposit - No Return," with David Niven and Don Knotts (one of the truly nice guys - he called me "Hanky," for some reason known only to him).

My last Disney film was "Cat From Outer Space." It had a good cast including Sandy Duncan, Ken Berry, Hans Conried, James Hampton, and Alan Young. The "M.A.S.H." contingent was represented by Harry Morgan and McLean Stevenson. Harry, who was so wonderful as Col. Sherman Potter on that TV classic, at first thought he would be working with veteran character actor *Henry* Jones (so good in "Vertigo" and "The Bad Seed"). When I showed up and was introduced to him, Harry confided, "Oh I'm so glad it's *you*, Hank. Henry's a bit mad, you know." Amusingly enough, after years of getting the other Henry Jones's residual checks by mistake and vice versa, I finally ran into him at the Mormon Genealogical Library in Westwood of all places, where he too was climbing his family tree.

McLean was a nice guy, easy to be around. We had several good scenes together, and he loved to spin yarns between takes about some of his show business pals ("Mickey Rooney is certifiable," he once told me - whatever that means). Ronnie Schell was in the cast too. We go way back to Don Sherwood-San Francisco days, and he still takes pleasure in being billed as "The World's Slowest Rising Comedian." And thanks to cast-mate Roddy McDowell - what a prince of a fellow he was - I am only one degree of separation from Kevin Bacon!

I played completely against my usual Disney type in "Cat From Outer Space." Instead of being a nebbish or a wimp, I was a pushy and loud army officer whose only mission in life was to make things miserable for Ken Berry and his cat. I screamed and yelled at my troops until I was finally "frozen" in my tracks via the magic of the cat's supernatural powers. Ah, another slice of Disney reality. By the way, eleven cats, all dyed to look the same, played the title role.

"LET'S PUT IT OVER WITH GROVER" - BIG MUSICAL NUMBER WITH
HANK JONES, WALLY COX, & THE CLEVELAND SUPPORTERS IN "THE FAMILY BAND"

"THE FAMILY BAND" FINALE: BUDDY EBSEN, JOHN DAVIDSON, WALTER BRENNAN,
LESLEY ANN WARREN, GOLDIE JEANNE HAWN, & HANK JONES (AMONG OTHERS)

FIGHTING WITH JOHN DAVIDSON IN "THE FAMILY BAND"

HANK JONES TRIES TO ANNOY JOHN DAVIDSON
(& EVERYONE ELSE) IN DISNEY'S "THE FAMILY BAND"

HANK JONES & WALLY COX IN BETWEEN A
YOUNG KURT RUSSELL & GOLDIE JEANNE HAWN
IN THE DISNEY MUSICAL "THE FAMILY BAND"

WALT DISNEY PRODUCTIONS

SHOOTING CALL

PICTURE "FAMILY BAND"   NO. 2198   DIRECTOR MICHAEL O'HERLIHY

SHOOTING CALL 9A   DATE THURSDAY MAY 4 1967

STAGE #4

INT BOWER BARN   "FAMILY BAND"   SC. 3.
INT BOWER BARN   "TEN FEET OFF THE GROUND"   CONTINUED.

REHEARSAL   ZORRO PLAZA

CAST	CHARACTER	1ST CALL	ON SET
X WALTER BRENNAN	GRANDPA	WN	
X BUDDY EBSEN	PAPA	8A	9A
X JANET BLAIR	MAMA	7A	9A
X LESLEY ANN WARREN	ALICE	7A	9A
X JOHN DAVIDSON	JOE	10A RHSL	WN
X RICHARD DEACON	MR. WRENN	10A RHSL	
X WALLY COX	MR. WAMPLER	10A RHSL	
X HANK JONES	DELIVERY BOY	10A RHSL	
X GOLDIE JEANNE HAWN	GIGGLY GIRL	10A RHSL	
X STEVE HARMON	ERNIE	10A RHSL	
X KURT RUSSELL	SIDNEY	830A	9A
X DEBBIE SMITH	LULU	830A	9A
X SMITTY WORDES	NETTIE	830A	9A
X HEIDI ROOK	ROSE	830A	9A
X JON WALMSLEY	QUINN	830A	9A
X PAMELYN FERDIN	LAURA	830A	9A
X BOBBY RIHA	MAYO	830A	9A

CHOREOGRAPHERS DANCEINS ETC			
X HUGH LAMBERT	CHOREOGRAPHER	10A RHSL	
X ROBERTA KEITH	ASST CHOREOGRAPHER	10A RHSL	
X	6 DANCEINS	10A RHSL	
X	14 DANCERS	10A RHSL	

ATMOS. STANDINS, ETC.			
X JOE PHILLIPS	SI BRENNAN		8A
X CHARLES McQUARY	SI EBSEN		8A
X	SI BLAIR		8A
X	SI WARREN		8A
X	5 SI'S (MINORS)		8A
X	SI DAVIDSON		WN
X HAROLD MINNIEAR	WELFARE WORKER		830A

ADVANCE SCHEDULE

FRIDAY MAY 5 (35TH DAY): _____   WESTERN ST
EXT RAPID CITY STREET   (D) PARTS 131 THRU 147.

TUESDAY THRU FRIDAY - MAY 9 THRU 12-
(36TH THRU 39TH DAYS): _____   WESTERN ST
RAPID CITY STREET   (D) COMPLETION.

RELAXING WITH JOHN DAVIDSON BETWEEN TAKES ON "THE FAMILY BAND"

REHEARSING THE DANCING FOR "WEST OF THE WIDE MISSOURI" WITH WALLY COX, RICHARD DEACON, & THE GANG IN "THE FAMILY BAND"

WITH THE ONE & ONLY JOHN CRAIG

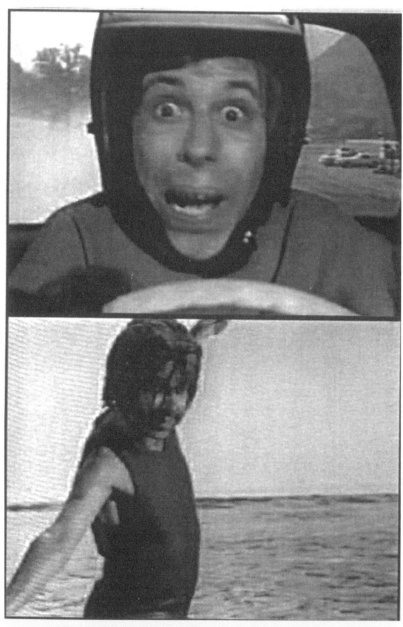

TWO ROLES IN WALT DISNEY'S "HERBIE RIDES AGAIN":
AS "SIR LANCELOT THE RACER" & AS "THE SURFER DUDE"

*AS A POOR COP BEING DELUGED WITH BANANAS (AH, METHOD ACTING!)
IN WALT DISNEY'S "NO DEPOSIT - NO RETURN"*

*A BE-FEATHERED TIM CONWAY AND HANK JONES IN
WALT DISNEY'S "THE SHAGGY D.A."*

WITH MCLEAN STEVENSON IN "CAT FROM OUTER SPACE"

SINGER/ACTOR MEL CARTER GETS THE CAT'S MAGIC NECKBAND FROM HIS SUPERIOR OFFICER IN WALT DISNEY'S "CAT FROM OUTER SPACE"

"THAT DARN CAT FROZE ME IN MY TRACKS"
WITH MCLEAN STEVENSON IN WALT DISNEY'S "CAT FROM OUTER SPACE"

A STUDY IN SUSPICION IN "CAT FROM OUTER SPACE"

LEADING THE TROOPS TO VICTORY IN "CAT FROM OUTER SPACE"

GIVING A HARD TIME TO KEN BERRY AND THE REAL STAR OF THE
MOVIE IN WALT DISNEY'S "CAT FROM OUTER SPACE"

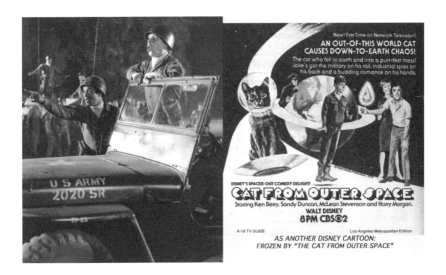

AS ANOTHER DISNEY CARTOON:
FROZEN BY "THE CAT FROM OUTER SPACE"

SIT-COMS & OTHER WORKS OF ART

I did lots of television shows in those early days of finding my way and trying my wings. One I'll never forget was early in 1964 on ABC-TV's "Day In Court." The casting director was looking for someone with a familiar TV face to play a teen idol whose parents were battling over all the money in his trust fund. This was *live* television, broadcast throughout the country as we actually did it. In the courtroom segment, I just sat there while my folks loudly squabbled back and forth about who got my money. It built slowly and finally reached a feverish pitch as the intensity of the scene increased. Finally, after being silent the whole show, I couldn't stand their arguments any longer. I jumped to my feet and cried out for all America to hear, "You're nothing but a vunch of bultures!"

They never asked me back on that program - I wonder why?

I filmed eight episodes of MGM's high school drama "Mr. Novak" about the same time. Even though I was 24 years old, I still looked about 16. Real 16-year-old actors could only work a few hours a day and had to attend school on the studio lot; so by hiring me to play the younger roles, MGM saved a lot of hassle and time. The title role was played the popular James Franciscus, who also starred other series such as "Longstreet" and "Naked City." Both Dean Jagger and Burgess Meredith played the principal of the school at different times. I usually had pretty small parts on these episodes, but they were great learning experiences and paid the bills. In one episode, "Penguin in My Garden," I had a scene with one of Alfred Hitchcock's leading ladies, Vera Miles, who played a nun. One day we shot well into lunchtime, and everyone was getting hungry and cranky. I remember Miss Miles, modestly dressed in her black nun's habit, swinging her big gold cross around over her chest in a wide circle and kvetching for all to hear, "Son of bitch, it's getting late - where's our frigging food?"

Jim Franciscus was a sharp looking nice guy and such a good actor. Little did I know working with him way back then that his daughter Kori, an offspring of his marriage to director William Wellman's daughter Kitty, would be my daughter Amanda's best friend in their early teens. Eventually, Jim divorced Kitty and unfortunately kind of went off the deep end

170

into substance abuse. I remember receiving late-night, somewhat incoherent phone calls from him in the late 1980s asking me for advice about how to raise our kids. Sadly, Jim died in 1991, much too young, but he certainly left an impressive body of work behind for us all.

Another show I enjoyed doing was "Nanny & The Professor," starring Juliet Mills and Richard Long. The particular episode we filmed, "Nanny On Wheels," was unique in that they made a three-dimensional "Viewmaster" reel of the show. Remember those? I adored Juliet Mills - what a sweetheart (I had a crush on her, I must say). Her father, John Mills, played the lead in one of my favorite movies of all times, David Lean's dark adaptation of Charles Dicken's "Great Expectations." Juliet (and her sister Hayley) was on the set when her Dad made that film and regaled me with her memories of the shoot in England. She's working still today and has a lead character role on the NBC soap opera "Passions."

Also on the "Nanny & The Professor" was Charles Lane, one of those character actors where you say, "Oh I don't know his name, but I sure know his face!" Skinny, hatchet-faced, bespectacled Mr. Lane was in literally hundreds of movies and is best known for his memorable roles in such Frank Capra classics as "It's A Wonderful Life," "Arsenic & Old "Lace," "You Can't Take It With You," and "Mr. Smith Goes To Washington." I was *so* honored to appear on screen with him, and did I ever learn a lot just watching him work. Charles Lane just celebrated his 100th birthday and is still an active member of Screen Actor's Guild. Amazing!

I became a resident of Hooterville in 1965 when I appeared in "Petticoat Junction" on CBS playing a friend of Bea Benaderet's daughter Linda Kaye Henning who was "Betty Jo" on the show. Bea had been a staple in radio for years on the Jack Benny and Burns & Allen programs and smoothly moved to television on this show as the owner of "The Shady Rest Hotel." Veteran actor Edgar Buchanan was "Uncle Joe." Edgar was familiarly known as "Doc," as he had played frontier doctors in scores of westerns and in real life had been a dentist himself. By the time we filmed "Petticoat Junction," he was pretty old and often was hard to awaken after falling asleep on the hotel couch between takes. All the other shows I did prior to "Petticoat" were filmed in black and white, and this was the first color program I ever did.

I did several episodes of the anthology series "Love American-Style." In one, I played the college roommate of my old "My Three Sons" friend Don Grady. Cute TV-staple-of-the-time Karen Valentine was also in it, portraying a co-ed assigned to our dorm by mistake. On another episode as "Weird Cousin Norman," I got a chance to do my bad Cary Grant impression while I tried to make time with Victoria Principal on a blind date. Needless-to-say, she wasn't crazy about going with me to the roller-skating rink. I told her skating "REALLY gives you the chills!" It was her loss. Victoria was a smart lady: at the time, besides acting, she also was an agent - and a good one. It follows then that even today she is hawking her own line of skin-care products on QVC and making a mint.

We shot "Love American-Style" at Paramount. I especially remember our lunches there at the studio commissary because we all would eat together with the cast of a new sci-fi series called "Star Trek." As we all enjoyed our cokes and hamburgers and shared our dreams, I don't think then that Bill Shatner, DeForest Kelley, or George Takei had any clue whatsoever that in 2006, far in the future, there would be conventions chock full of "Trekies" still honoring that show; and little did our other table-mates Greg Morris, Barbara Bain, and Marty Landau realize either that their new opus "Mission Impossible" would spawn three feature films far into the new millennium.

Another sit-com that was fun to do was one largely forgotten today: a CBS show called "Arnie," with Herschel Bernardi and Sue Ane Langdon. Herschel was a real *mensch* who got his start on the old Peter Gunn TV series and then went on to follow Zero Mostel as Tevye on Broadway and on the road in "Fiddler On The Roof." On "Arnie," I played a young lawyer, just out of law school, who finds himself arguing a case against real-life legendary barrister Melvin Belli, playing himself. Mr. Belli was San Francisco's most famous lawyer, a real dandy and bon vivant who had many famous clients, including Lee Harvey Oswald's killer Jack Ruby. I found him to be hammier than any of us professional hams all put together. He even wore his own cape to the studio for the court scene, for heaven's sake. The payoff in the script was that I actually won the case against him. Even though he was acting, I don't think Mr. Belli liked that at all.

I took a trip on the "Love Boat" too. In fact, I almost made lots and lots of voyages. When they cast the part of

"Gopher" on the program, I was in the final running for the role. Fred Grandy, with whom I often competed for commercial parts, got the gig; his high visibility on the show help him win a Iowa congressional election later on in life. I knew Fred would end up in Congress: he was the only actor I ever knew who always carried a black briefcase to every audition (Did you know Fred was best man in David Eisenhower's wedding to Julie Nixon?).

I played the part of the "Ships' Inspector" when the show was in the top ten rating-wise. When I showed up for filming, it was kind of funny because Gavin MacLeod, who played the Captain of "The Love Boat," ran over to the stage door in full uniform to welcome me "on board" - like he really was running a cruise. I didn't have the heart to tell him that we hadn't left port and were still on a soundstage in Culver City. Ahoy, Matey!

Some of the shows I performed in were filmed in front of a live studio audience like "The Jeffersons." The producers always got the audience rockin' and rollin' prior to the show by playing their lively theme song "We're Movin' On Up!" at full volume. The joint was jumpin' by the time filming started. It was quite a cast. Isabel Sanford, who was known on the set as "The Queen" and acted like one, played Louise Jefferson; I portrayed one of her fellow social workers where she worked. Roxie Roker was cast opposite Franklin Cover as Helen Willis in one of TV's first interracial marriages; Roxie herself was married to a Caucasian and was the mother of rock superstar Lenny Kravitz. Marla Gibbs played the sharp-tongued maid Florence Johnston, and had quite a wry sense of humor herself. But the real surprise to me was what Sherman Hemsley, who played volatile George Jefferson, was like offstage: he was the gentlest, soft-spoken man in real life - totally the opposite of his on-screen character. It's hard to join an already-established group midstream, and Sherman made me feel so welcome when I was cast on "The Jeffersons."

Once in a while I was cast completely against my type. I filmed some "Mod Squads" on ABC for producers Aaron Spelling and Harve Bennett. They hired me on the "A Is For Annie" episode to play a conniving and corrupt District Attorney just oozing slime. Boy, was that a blast! On another "Mod Squad," I was a young college student who was given LSD by his roommates at a party. That rat Billy Dee Williams, later of

"Mahogany" and "Star Wars" fame," was one of the culprits who did me in. I had a big death scene that had to filmed in one take as I had to reel around the dorm knocking over everything in my path as I bit the dust. I managed to do it and even got some applause from the hardened crew watching. Little did they know that I didn't know what the hell I was doing: I just said a quick prayer, went for it, and hoped we got it on the first go-round. Thank God we did - I didn't want to have to pay for all that broken furniture.

Sometimes the scripts were beyond belief. I filmed an episode of NBC's "Emergency" once that really shows what I mean. I played a young man who was driving his car routinely on the freeway until a pretty redhead in a sports car cut him off. Both autos flipped over, causing paramedics Randolph Mantooth and Kevin Tighe to come to our rescue. After having temper tantrums that could be heard all over Universal Studios, the girl and I stopped our yelling at each other and started conversing in a more civilized way. Gradually, we learned we both were interested in architecture ("Who do you like best - Neutra or Frank Lloyd Wright?") and the chemistry started cooking. At the end of the show, after literally nearly killing each other, we walked off into the sunset together hand in hand ... just like in real life.

You always hear about temperament and ego when it comes to big stars. Phooey! Not in my experience. I know it sounds saccharine, but - truly - I've found that the bigger they are, the nicer they are. All those years of fond "people memories" prove it. There was the time I was to film a TV show with Henry Fonda. It was called "The Smith Family" and also had Ronnie Howard and Janet Blair in it. I didn't know what to expect, working with a living legend of that magnitude. I'm afraid I arrived on the set with trepidation, trembling in my boots a bit. Fortunately, his make-up artist, John Inzerella, was a good friend of mine and had told him that I was coming. When I arrived for make-up, Mr. Fonda sat in an adjoining chair and put me at ease by saying, "Hi, Hank. I'm a 'Hank' too ... just call me that, and we'll get along fine."

And I did ... and we did!

One of my most memorable jobs was playing Ringo Starr's twin brother in an NBC-TV musical version of Mark Twain's classic novel "The Prince And The Pauper." We had a terrific cast: nice-guy John Ritter, Carrie Fisher straight out of

"Star Wars," George Harrison strumming away while his guitar gently wept, Art Carney - forever Ed Norton, beautiful Angie Dickinson, and mega-movie-villain Vincent Price. Vincent had to be one of the sweetest men in the world off camera. I told him how he had scared the bejeezus out of me when I saw him in 3-D in "House of Wax" when I was a kid. Vincent rubbed his hands together and replied with a cackle and in a sinister voice, "Oh I hope so!"

I was "Ognir Rrats" on the show (guess what that spells backwards?). After nearly five hours of make-up every day, I was a dead-ringer for Ringo. It was uncanny. I looked so much like him that some days I would go to the NBC Commissary as "Ringo" and fool the other lunch-goers into thinking I was him while the real deal stayed back in his dressing room eating in privacy. As we got to know each other, I learned that Ringo actually preferred people calling him "Richard Starkey," his real name: "Ringo," I think he felt, was a commodity, and "Richard" was a genuine person. Absolutely stunning women were on the prowl for him and would try and slip him their room keys or phone numbers. It happened all the time. Now I know this sounds like a true male fantasy, but when it goes on and on and one realizes that these ladies weren't interested in "Richard" at all but in "Ringo" as a trophy, it was very sad to see. In between takes, Ringo would play me songs he had written - not to show off, but just to see what I thought of them because he knew I had been in music too. Honestly, they weren't very good, and I kind of felt he somehow was trying desperately to get out from under the shadow of Lennon and McCartney's more proven talents by attempting to write music himself. That show was an arduous shoot, but for a month - hey, I was a BEATLE!

I guess I should have a tee-shirt made that says "I survived Robin Williams." I played the funnyman's defense attorney when the court was trying to commit him to an insane asylum on the one-hour special edition of ABC's "Mork & Mindy." As I said earlier, in my mind, along with Peter Ustinov, Robin is one of the few actors who truly could be called "a genius." But oh my Lord - he wore you out! Robin was ALWAYS "on." He did the dress rehearsal of the show in some obscure Serbian dialect. He used the script as a base line to do his comic riffs - and they usually were funnier than the original lines. I've never seen anyone who had so many choices of where he could take you - and sometimes it was a bumpy ride. Robin is very much a child, and I mean that in the kindest sense. He somehow can tap into the kid in all of us and make it work. I remember going back to his dressing room with him and playing a selection of brand new kids' computer games. He won every time. But there's one feather in my cap I'll treasure forever: I actually made HIM break up. As his attorney, I gave a very sardonic, disgusted reading to the line, "I'M his lawyer. The COURT appointed me" like it was the worst fate that could have befallen me. He gave a loud snort, pounded the table, and guffawed for a good half-minute. I got him! I wouldn't trade that moment for anything.

I did quite a few episodes on ABC's "The Patty Duke Show" playing one of her high school friends and occasional dates. That was the show where she played two look-alike teenaged girls: Patty who was typically very American, and Cathy who was her more dignified British cousin. In one of the scripts, the two traded places while on a date with me, and I had to figure out who was who. The confusion led to some nice comic moments, the film of which in turn happily led me to more acting jobs on other shows. One of the joys of that program was getting to work on film with my real-life friend, Eddie Applegate who played Patty's boyfriend "Richard." Eddie and I have remained close pals now for forty-plus years. It's really quite amazing how neither one of us have physically changed even the slightest bit since those early days on the show. Oh ok - a wrinkle here, a receding hairline there, a bit of gray ...

The producer of the "Patty Duke Show" was an old-time radio guy named Bob Sweeney. Bob often hired semi-retired stars from that medium to guest on the show. On one episode, I was featured with Harold Peary who used to play "The Great Gildersleeve" on radio and later in movies. We hit it off immediately because Mr. Peary also grew up in San Leandro like I did. He knew my mother's father Fred Schmidt who had a feed & fuel store there. San Leandro had a large Portuguese community, and Harold Peary was one of their most successful sons. I loved to hear his patented Gildersleeve laugh on the set, and he even threw in his trademarked exasperated radio phrase, "LEROY!!" once in a while.

When I filmed those shows in the 60s, I had no idea of the turmoil Patty Duke was going through. Although somewhat tense and uptight, she otherwise seemed a pretty normal teenager. But in reality she had been yanked from her real family years before by her "managers" the Rosses and instructed to have no contact with them. The Rosses told her what to do and made Patty pretty much a puppet to their every whim. Only years later after going through absolute hell in her personal life, severing her relationship with the Rosses, and eventually diagnosing and then treating what turned out to be bi-polar disorder did Patty emerge as the squared-away, happy, and healthy woman she is today. What a journey she has had and now what a wonderful outcome. Good for her!

Virginia Martindale was casting director on several Don Fedderson productions like "My Three Sons" and was instrumental in getting me work on some of their other shows. "Family Affair" was another Fedderson product, and it starred Brian Keith as "Uncle Bill," Sebastian Cabot as the huffy butler "Mr. French," Kathy Garver as "Cissy," Johnny Whitaker as "Jody," and little Anissa Jones as "Buffy." I played Cissy's delivery-boy boyfriend "Johnny Archer." Brian Keith was a reserved, quiet guy who spoke ever so softly. When we had scenes filmed together in a two shot, he was easy to work with - no problem. But sometimes for my own close-up in the same scene, Mr. K. didn't hang around to feed me my off-camera lines; as in "My Three Sons" with Fred MacMurray, the script girl said Brian's dialogue to which I would then respond with my lines. Unfortunately, this young lady was no where near as good at getting the feel of the lines as was Del, her counterpart on "My Three Sons." She spoke in a normal tone of voice, not super-soft as did Brian. So I was mortified when the program finally hit the air, and I saw the scenes that I did with Brian Keith. As they cut back and forth between us on our close-ups, I'm shouting my lines, and he's whispering his. It didn't work at all. Lessons learned: I should have paid more attention to the way he delivered his lines and remembered that during my close-ups.

I would never want my child to be a kid-actor. They are made to act as adults when they're still only just children. It's not right, and it's not fair. About the only two of that breed with whom I worked who turned out really well were Ronnie Howard and Kurt Russell. Ronnie's parents, Rance and Jean Howard, were both in the business and down-to-earth, really good people. They saw all the pressures and problems child-actors faced and were determined not to let them happen to their kids Ronnie and Clint. Ronnie was not allowed to play "star" - Rance and Jean saw he remained just the kid he really was. I remember playing catch between scenes with all the Howards on the Columbia Ranch lot, and it was as if we were in Des Moines, Iowa on a Saturday afternoon rather than on a Hollywood studio back-lot. Kurt's Dad Bing Russell did the same thing, with a no-nonsense "you're just a kid, not a star" attitude towards his son. Kurt turned out well too, just like Ronnie. By the way, just who is this "Ron Howard" who's directing all these important movies of late? He *can't* be little Ronnie. Ronnie had hair!

But poor Anissa Jones, our little "Buffy" on "Family Affair," didn't get the same happy ending to her life as Ronnie and Kurt. She died at the age of 18 in 1976 from what the coroner said was "one of the most severe cases of drug overdose" he had ever seen. So sad - it shouldn't have happened. Adding even more of a tragic finish to the story, Brian Keith, Anissa's beloved "Uncle Bill" on the show, was a suicide himself. He died by his own hand in 1997 as was trying to cope with terminal respiratory illness and the recent gunshot suicide of his daughter, Daisy, only ten weeks before.

God bless them all.

HANK JONES
TV IN THE STONE AGE

**Hank Jones, Don Grady,
William Frawley** and **Gail Gilmore** in
"My Three Sons"

Patty Duke and **Hank Jones** in
"The Patty Duke Show"

Minnie Pearl and **Hank Jones** on
*"The Tennessee
Ernie Ford Show"*

Hank Jones and **Victoria Principal** in
"Love American Style"

September 29, 1972

Dear Hank,

Thanks for being with us on LOVE, AMERICAN STYLE."

It was one of those parts that had to sell fast but couldn't bang it on the nose, and you did very well.

Thanks for walking the good taste tight rope for us.

We look forward to seeing you again on our show.

Best regards,

Jim and Arnold

Mr. Hank Jones
North Hollywood, California

W. A. __1298__

Series __MOD SQUAD__
Producer __HARVE BENNETT__
Director __BOB LEWIS__
Title __A IS FOR ANNIE__
Prod. No. __3/00 4 · 056__

CALL SHEET

Day __THURSDAY - 6 - 25 - 70__
__5__ Day out of __7__ days
Reh. or Lv. Call __730 a__
Shooting Call __8:00 a__
Location __STAGE 24__

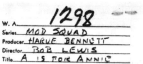

SET # SET	SCENES	CAST	D/N	PAGES	LOCATION
INT MCKENNA LIVING ROOM	41 - 47 - 48	6·7·9·10·13	N	2 4/8	STAGE 24
INT MCKENNA LIVING ROOM	80 - 81	1·2·6·7·9·10·1·13·13	D	1 3/8	" "
INT. SIMPSONS OFFICE	52·53·54·55	1·9·10·11·12	D	7/8	" 23
INT. SIMPSONS OFFICE	32	9·10·11	D	1 4/8	" "
INT SIMPSONS OFFICE	17	10·11	D	1	" "
				7 2/8	

CAST & DAY PLAYERS	PART OF	MAKE-UP/LEAVE	SET CALL	REMARKS
1 MICHAEL COLE	PETE	10:00 a	10:30	
2 CLARENCE WILLIAMS	LINC	10:00 a	10:30	
3 PEGGY LIPTON	JULIE	H	H	
4 TIGE ANDREWS	ADAM	H	H	
5 MISS VAN FLEET	ANNIE	H	H	
6 CINDY EILBACHER	SALLY	730 a	8:00 a	
7 JEWEL BLANCH	LUANNE	730 a	8:00 a	
9 RON HAYES	MCKENNA	730 a	8:00 a	
10 EDMUND GILBERT	SIMPSON	730 a	8:00 a	
11 HANK JONES	HERBIE HUGHES	10:00 a	10 30 a	
12 ROBERT CLEAVES (NEW)	ROY SANDERS	10:00 a	10 30 a	
13 BARBARA BOLES	MRS MCKENNA	70:0 a	8:00 a	
RON RONDELL	STUNT COORD	H		
ALAN OLINEY	DBL LINC	H		

ATMOSPHERE AND STANDINS		SPECIAL INSTRUCTIONS
Standins - LIBBY·PATTY·JOE·CHRIS·ELMER	7.30 a	
1 WELFARE WORKER - AS ORDERED	7.30 a	
25 ATMOS - AS ORDERED		(5 AT 1030 AM - 20 AT 11:30 AM)

ADVANCE SHOOTING NOTES				
SHOOTING DATE	SET NO.	SET NAME	LOCATION	SCENE NO.
FRIDAY		INT SCHOOL ROOM	STAGE 23	1·2·24·4·100...

FAMED ATTORNEY MELVIN BELLI MEETS HIS MATCH ON CBS'S "ARNIE"

*WITH KEVIN TIGHE & RANDOLPH MANTOOTH
ON NBC-TV'S "EMERGENCY"*

HENRY FONDA & HANK JONES ON ABC-TV'S "THE SMITH FAMILY"
"JUST CALL ME 'HANK' AND WE'LL GET ALONG FINE"

PAM DAWBER, CONRAD JANIS, ROBIN WILLIAMS, & HANK JONES
IN ABC-TV'S "MORK & MINDY"

*BILL YARMY, ROBIN WILLIAMS, & A BELEAGUERED HANK JONES
"MORK & MINDY"*

ROBIN WILLIAMS AS "MORK" MOONS HANK JONES AS HIS "DEFENSE ATTORNEY"

Ringo Starr, Hank Jones (as Ognir Rrats) and Carrie Fisher in "Ringo"

IT TOOK FIVE HOURS OF MAKE-UP EVERY DAY,
BUT I GOT TO BE "A BEATLE" FOR A WHOLE MONTH!!

(TOP) GETTING THE FINAL MAKEUP TOUCHES AS "RINGO"
(BOTTOM) REHEARSING WITH RINGO (IN MIDDLE) & SEYMOUR CASSELL

STUDIO CENTER
CALL SHEET

UNIT
6TH DAY OF SHOOTING

SERIES *"FAMILY AFFAIR"*
PRODUCER *EDMUND HARTMANN*

8A SHOOTING ~~OR LEAVING CALL~~

8022—

DATE *MONDAY 20 MAY 1968*

PICT. *"A WALTZ FROM VIENNA" (0135-WFV)*

NO. *W 73*   DIRECTOR *CHARLES BARTON*

SET				SCS.	CAST	LOC.
SET *INT ENTRY HALL (0135-WFV)*	(D)	2 3/8	SCS.	20	1-2-3-4-5	LOC. *STAGE 12*
SET *INT ENTRY HALL (0135-WFV)*	(D)	1 7/8	SCS.	42	1-2-3-45-41	LOC.
SET *INT ENTRY HALL (0135-WFV)*	(N)	4/8	SCS.	16	1	LOC.
SET *INT LIVING ROOM (0135-WFV)*	(N)	2 4/8	SCS.	17-18-19	1-2-3	LOC.
SET *INT LIVING ROOM (0135-WFV)*	(D)	4/8	SCS.	11	1-2	LOC.
SET *INT KITCHEN (0135-WFV)*	(D)	2 3/8	SCS.	12	1-2- 41	LOC.
SET *INT KITCHEN (0135-WFV)*	(D)	7/8	SCS.	10	2 - 41	LOC.

	CAST AND DAY PLAYERS	PART OF	MAKEUP	SET CALL	REMARKS
1	BRIAN KEITH	BILL	7:30A	8A	
2	SEBASTIAN CABOT	FRENCH	7:30A	8A	
3	KATHY GARVER	CISSY	6:30	8A	
4	ANISSA JONES	BUFFY	—	8A	
5	JOHN WHITAKER	JODY	—	8A	
41	HANK JONES (NEW)	JOHNNY	9:0 DA	9:30	

ATMOSPHERE AND STANDINS			THRU GATE		
STANDINS AS REQUIRED			7:45A		

ADVANCE SCHEDULE

7TH DAY TUESDAY 21 MAY 1968
NEW YORK STREET
EXT VIA VENETO SIDEWALK CAFE (0131-CUB) Sc. 2 (D) 1 4/8
MOVE TO STAGE 12
INT JODYS BEDROOM (0132-BAW) Sc. 39 (D) 1 7/8
INT DEN (0130-YFJ) Sc. 43 (D) 1 1/8
EXT VILLA GARDENS (0131-CUB) Sc. 18 (N) 2
INT VILLA LIVING ROOM (0131-CUB) Sc. 30-32-34-36 (N) 1 3/8
INT VILLA LIVING ROOM (0131-CUB) Sc. 46 (D) 2 3/8

8TH DAY WEDNESDAY 22 MAY 1968
INT BILL'S ROOM (0135-WFV) Sc. 22 (N) 2 4/8
INT CISSY + BUFFY ROOM (0136-CLE) Sc. 18-19 (N) 1 4/8
INT CISSY + BUFFY ROOM (0136-CLE) Sc. 42-43 (N) 4/8
INT CISSY + BUFFY ROOM (0140-NAS) Sc. 16-17-18 (D) 2 7/8
INT BILL'S OFFICE (0138-OLI) Sc. 20 (D) 7/8
INT BILLS OFFICE (0138-OLI) Sc. 36 (D) 1 7/8
INT BILLS OFFICE (0138-OLI) Sc. 46 (D) 5/8

ASST. DIR *JOHN GAUDIOSO — RICHARD LEARMAN*   PROD. MGR *John B. ___*

WITH SUSANNE & SAMMY JACKSON

Sammy Jackson

NO TIME FOR SERGEANTS & SAMMY

I often auditioned for various pilots of prospective television shows. One experience I'll never forget was when I was up for the second lead, "Ben," in the TV version of the Broadway hit, "No Time For Sergeants."

On Broadway, the lead role of country bumpkin Will Stockdale was played by the marvelous Andy Griffith. The TV program's Will was my soon-to-be good friend Sammy Jackson, a handsome country-boy from Henderson, North Carolina; he was a mutual friend of my pal Diane Beach, who I lived next door to in my Hollywood apartment days. Hoyt Bowers, the casting director at Warner Brothers, thought I would be a natural for Sammy's sidekick and set up a meeting with the producer of the show, Gracie's beloved George Burns.

But first I had to do a screen test for the role. At that time, the head of TV production at Warner Brothers was Jack Webb, who had honed his producer's chops over the years as star and the man behind the ultra-successful police drama "Dragnet." After a few days pouring over my script and trying to incorporate some of the comedy shtick that I had successfully used in past roles, I went in to meet Mr. Webb. I found him to be warm and friendly, unlike his stiff "Joe Friday" personage on film. We had something in common to talk about, as we both had Bay Area show business roots and enjoyed reminiscing about those days that were golden to us both.

We then walked to the huge soundstage where Jack introduced me to Efrem Zimbalist, Jr., then star of the popular "77 Sunset Strip" show, who was just hanging around to watch my test. After the set was dressed and the lights were lit, we started filming; but after a few takes Jack Webb began to frown and ordered the cameras to stop rolling. He told me to hold back on all the vocal inflections I was using and cut way down on any animation I was bringing to the part. In other words, pull back and "dull it up." He was the director. I thought he knew what would be best, so I somewhat reluctantly complied. We completed the screen test just the way Mr. Webb asked me to do it.

A few days later, I went to the old General Services Studio in Hollywood to meet with George Burns. I entered his offices and found him surrounded by his long-time cronies and writers at a big table. Burns was wearing a beret and an ascot, looking very much in charge. After finishing up fine-tuning a couple of gags, his first words to me were, "Who the f**k are you?" Everybody in the room laughed except me: I was shocked and hurt. I didn't know what to say. After the uproar died down, Burns said to me, "I saw your test. You sounded more like the sergeant than the kid. I don't think it's going to work." I was dumbfounded. I had only acted that way because Jack Webb had insisted that I do it like that. But what could I really say? There it was on film for all to see, with me acting like Joe Friday instead of Ben Whitledge. I said a quiet "Thank you, Mr. Burns" and left.

Kevin O'Neal, brother of Ryan, eventually got the role of Ben. Sammy Jackson never really got along with him and said he always wished that I had gotten the part instead. But that's show biz. It was just a passing incident for me. But the real tragedy of "No Time For Sergeants" was yet to come; and it wasn't mine ... it was Sammy's. Sammy was making more money than he ever dreamed of. He helped support many of his poor relatives back in North Carolina - they seemed to come out of the woodwork as the program grew in popularity. The sharks and the "yes-men" arrived and surrounded him. He was on the cover *TV Guide* and his face was everywhere. He co-starred with Roy Orbison in a movie called, "The Fastest Guitar In The West" and did a TV pilot, "Rhubarb," where he was billed above the title with Groucho himself. Sinatra gave him a choice role and directed him in "None But The Brave," and he hung out with Elvis and lots of other big stars. He fell in love with his Sergeant's leading lady, Lori Sebald, and the affair was blooming. Life for Sammy was good - no, it was GREAT!

But then, in a textbook example that nothing lasts forever in show business, poor Sammy Jackson's success abruptly ended. Here's what happened: at that time, ABC had two shows on the air produced by George Burns, Sammy's "No Time For Sergeants" and one with Connie Stevens in which Burns also appeared called "Wendy & Me." The brass at the network gave Burns a choice: only one of his shows could remain on the air, and he had to pick which one. For Burns, the choice was easy: he decided to go with the one in which he co-starred with Connie Stevens. And so, even though "No Time For Sergeants" had a high rating as one of the top twenty programs on the air, it was cancelled quick as a flash.

The way Sammy Jackson found out how he was a man without a show still makes me squirm. Sammy had to fly to Lake Tahoe to make a personal appearance for the network. He was leaving the ABC Hollywood Studios at Prospect and Tallmadge in his spiffy new sports car to go to the airport. As he approached the main gate of the studio, the guard there said, "Mr. Jackson, I have to confiscate your airplane tickets. Your show has been cancelled." With that, the guard grabbed the tickets from Sammy's hand and motioned him off the lot. Can you believe that?

After a stint as a radio disc jockey on L.A.'s KLAC and a short stay in Nashville, the downward spiral in Sammy Jackson's life continued. He could find little work. His girl friend left him, and he began to drink heavily and brood a lot. Most of his friends who clung around him as a star disappeared when things went south. Poor Sammy would spend hours many nights in his darkened apartment just watching old 16mm films of his past "No Time For Sergeant's" shows, mumbling his lines to himself. I often would be awakened in the early hours by telephone calls from him, blearily asking me, "Hanker, what went wrong?" He eventually married a lovely woman named Susanne, and, for a time, things looked up; but still no work to speak of was forthcoming, and they had sell their lovely horse-farm in Agora Hills and move to Las Vegas. He tried so hard to make ends meet, but eventually Sammy ended up as a security guard at one of the Vegas casinos. After years of trying to battle his drinking problem and life's misfortunes, one morning, they found him in his bed - dead. *Variety*, the show business newspaper, didn't even think he was "big" enough to print his obituary ... Sammy, a man who had his own TV show and was on the cover of *TV Guide* for God's sake!

Sammy Jackson, I think, just died of a broken heart. He was my good, dear friend, and I hope now he finally is at peace.

10-PERCENTERS & MANAGERS

"Bullets Durgom," "Swifty Lazar," "Leland Hayward:" these were all legendary ten-percenters or agents during Hollywood's Golden Era. For "talent," it was absolutely essential to have an agent and usually a manager in order to even get in the door of a studio to get a job.

I've been blessed with the best over the years. As I mentioned before, George Burke and Bill Weems were my first personal managers. They handled both Dean and me during the Ford Show years and then continued to represent me as an actor after Dean was drafted and I had to survive solo. Also in their stable of clients were Jim Backus, Kay Starr, Everett Sloan, Ed Ames, Carole Cook, and the singing team of Joe & Eddie.

Here's a bit about them all: Kay Starr, known around the office as "The First Lady of Song," was still in demand after all those years of hit records like "Side By Side" and "Wheel Of Fortune;" she was a ballsy broad, to put it in the vernacular, and had been around the block and then some. Carole Cook was Lucille Ball's comic protégé and can best be described as being "a hoot." After making a lousy throw with a tomahawk at the vulnerable part of a cardboard cowboy on Johnny Carson's "Tonight Show," Ed Ames's career was refueled after his old hits with his singing brothers with new chartbusters like "My Cup Runneth Over" and "The Impossible Dream;" coincidentally, Arlena Moslander, one of the Hank & Dean stalwart fans from way back, now runs The Ames Brothers' fan-club today. Everett Sloan was a valued member of Orson Wells' stock company, being in "Citizen Kane" and "The Lady From Shanghai;" sadly, he committed suicide while a client of George and Bill's. I went with George to visit Everett on the set of Jerry Lewis's "The Patsy" shortly before he died, and he wasn't a happy man. Joe Gilbert and Eddie Brown were a lively musical duo who made their mark on the "Danny Kaye Show" on CBS. Unfortunately, they had problems handling the pressures of success, and a troubled Joe was killed in a traffic accident in the mid-60s.

I especially liked hanging around Jim Backus. When I was a kid and he was on early TV's "I Married Joan," I had sent away for Jim's autographed picture that he inscribed, as per my warped instructions, "To Hank Jones & his hamster Cicero." I told you I was weird! Jim had played James Dean's father in "Rebel Without A Cause," and I loved hearing about what it was like to work with this true Hollywood rebel. Jim at the time was on TV's "Gilligan's Island" playing pompous Thurston Howell III. When he found out that I knew Stan Laurel, Jim was very eager have me take him down to Stan's Santa Monica apartment to meet the master; unfortunately, what I couldn't tell Jim was that Stan told me that he *hated* the "Gilligan" show, didn't think it was funny, and thought that Bob Denver and Alan Hale were stealing bits and pieces of business (badly) from Laurel & Hardy.

George and Bill were a great duo, each with his own strengths in getting the job done. George was the gregarious outgoing partner, while Bill was the more "hold 'em to the vest" type. However, once in a while if things were not going well in a particular negotiation, Bill would put on the dramatics to attain whatever contract perk he was after - earning him the well-deserved nickname of "Willie The Weep." On slow days between pictures and shows (and believe me there were many), I sometimes would just go over to George's office and play cribbage or gin while we waited for the phone to ring. Some days it did, some days it didn't.

One major role for a personal manager is to sign up his clients for good agency representation. George and Bill, having been agents themselves, knew them all, and I was fortunate when they placed me with the prestigious William Morris Agency in Beverly Hills. The Morris office was one of the nation's oldest talent bookers, starting way back in the vaudeville days and continuing on through the years covering all media and live performance venues. I had quite a crew to represent me there. The senior agents who tried to sell me were Elliott Wax, Phil Kellogg, and Norman Brokaw. They had me up for countless roles on shows in which the Morris office usually had a financial interest.

I well remember one morning when Norman took me to meet comic Joey Bishop, one of Sinatra's "Rat Pack," at his home in Beverly Hills. Joey had his own show, and they were looking for a young guy to play the nephew of his wife, Abby Dalton, on the program. When we arrived, Joey was still in his bathrobe and looked surprised to see us. He offered us breakfast, which we declined, and basically just did a "look-see" to decide if I would fit into his TV family. For two months or so, it looked like we might make a deal. In the end, however, the producers and Joey decided to scrap the whole idea of giving Abby a nephew, and I was out before I was in. That kind of stuff went on a lot, and it was tough getting used to the ups and downs of it all. Of all my agents at the Morris office in the 60s, only Norman Brokaw is still there now, some forty-five years later. He's their "senior senior" agent now and remains a real class act.

Some of the junior agents at William Morris who serviced me as a client were Roland Perkins, Bob Shapeiro, Gil Barnett, Mike Rosenfeld, Phil Kellogg, Ron DeBlasio, Irv Schechter, and Barry Diller. They all started in the mail room and nearly every one of them went on to found or play a part in other major agencies that would eventually threaten the dominance of the Morris office in the business. Barry Diller was something else, even early on. He was always well spoken, nattily dressed, and seemed much more like an aristocrat rather than a stereotypical slick 10-percenter. Marlo Thomas got him his first job at William Morris in the mailroom, and he quickly worked his way up to being a junior agent. We had a good relationship, and Barry got me quite a bit of work. On one occasion when I was shooting "No Time For Sergeants" at Warner Brothers, he came out to the studio to have lunch with me in the commissary. Unfortunately, I had to dine with Barry in my costume, which consisted of a dance-hall girl's scanty dress, pantyhose, and high heels. I was portraying a G.I. who was appearing in the camp show, and it was too hard to get out of the damn outfit at lunchtime knowing I had to put it on again right afterwards. I don't think Barry was very much at ease eating with Hank in drag: he kept looking around the dining room trying to hide and worrying about who was watching us. Another memory I have of him was when I returned from visiting Stan Laurel at his home, and Barry must have spent an hour asking me questions about what Mr. Hardy's partner was like. He was a fan too.

Barry Diller was too big for the William Morris Agency to contain. The wunderkind left and went on to an amazing career at ABC where he "invented" the TV movie, then ran Paramount and 20th Century Fox Studios, launched QVC Shopping Network, sold it and then bought Home Shopping Network. Barry has continued on buying and selling corporations and cable companies to this day and soon will own the world. Obviously, he owes everything about his huge success to me alone, and I'm still waiting for my cut of the profits. It may be a long wait.

The hard part of being an actor is that it's almost impossible to get a job directly yourself. To land a role in a picture or TV show, you have to bug your manager who then lights a fire under your agent who then submits you to the casting director who then shows your film to the director who then gets the approval of the producer. WHEW! If any part of this chain is weak, then you don't get the job. The whole process can be very frustrating - and it was.

I made good money for the William Morris Agency, but probably not enough. When their interest waned, George and Bill signed me with General Artists Corporation where they both had been agents themselves. They had a good group there too including Sandy Gallin, "Slick George" Spelvin, Joel Briskin, Max Arno, Norton Stein, Bud Moss, Jack Gilardi, and Jerry Steiner (Sandy went on to manage Dolly Parton, Jack married Annette Funicello, and Jerry married singer Joanie Somers and sadly died very young).

George Burke began to show signs of serious illness in 1966 and was not able to function as well as he had in the past. It was so sad seeing what was happening to this good man, but I gradually realized that George wasn't getting any better. I had to wrestle long and hard about leaving Burke & Weems Management. It was a difficult decision to make and carry out because I had grown to love George and his family so much. By the time "Blackbeard's Ghost" was ready to be released by Disney in 1967, I had hired the p.r. firm of Mann Scharf & Associates to handle my press relations and publicize the three films I had under my theatrical belt. When I finally did move on from George, Mann called well-known personal manager Mimi Weber and asked if she might be interested in representing me. She was, and soon I was in the stable of actors in Mimi Weber Management.

Mimi was and is one of the most savvy personal managers in the business; indeed the Conference of Personal Managers West elected her several times to high offices in their prestigious organization. She started as an agent with MCA, and then moved out on her own. She first handled George Maharis, very popular in his heyday on the "Route 66" series. When she signed me to a management contract, her other clients included Nick Nolte, Harry Guardino, Chris Stone, Jayne Meadows, singer

Johnny Desmond, and character actors Art Metrano and Logan Ramsey, just to name a few. Mimi made us feel like we were "family," and we were to her - it was mutual. Mimi knew everybody. She dated Cary Grant, palled around with Steve and Eydie, and was a good friend of Sinatra (whom she called "Francis"). In fact, when Old Blue Eyes was appearing near our San Diego home, Mimi simply called his "Girl Friday," Dorothy, and we ended up in the Sinatra house seats with a ringside view. Mimi's best girlfriend was Myrna Loy - such a kind and classy lady - and I remember how both Mimi and Myrna were counting the days waiting for my daughter Amanda to be born in 1973.

She did have a good perspective on the business side of show-biz, however: over her desk, Mimi had a sign that read "Remember - it was an actor who killed Lincoln." That axiom held a bit of truth for Mimi some years back when she had to sue Nick Nolte, who was hotter than hot from his "Rich Man, Poor Man" mini-series to "The Deep" and "Down & Out In Beverly Hills."   Nick owed Mimi lots of $$$ for back commissions which he didn't pay. I thought that just plain stunk because Mimi had worked her tail off to get him where he was - a major star. I will say Nick was always very friendly to me, however. I remember one of Mimi's parties at her beautiful home chatting cordially with Nick, but trying futilely to keep my eyes off his main squeeze - a lovely young thing known only as "Legs" who, I may say unequivocally, lived up to her name.

Mimi did find happiness with her client Pam Dawber, however, and it couldn't have worked out better for them both. Pam, after her days starring with Robin Williams on "Mork & Mindy," became much in demand for TV movies and went on to other series, such as "My Sister Sam." Thanks to Mimi's skills as a manager and Pam's talents as an actress, her career soared. Although Pam has cut back of late due to her marriage to Mark Harmon and motherhood, the Dawber-Weber relationship has endured and thrived. Like Pam, all of us who were clients of Mimi Weber owe her a great debt. We couldn't have survived so well without her.

As I grew older, Mimi placed me with a few other agencies that specialized more in character actors. This was a good move, because unless you became a star, an actor had to fight like hell to be noticed at a major agency like William Morris or GAC. Middle-sized agents like Fred Amsel at Kumin-Olenick

Agency and Sue Goldin at Goldin-Dennis Agency got me good parts in my 30s and 40s. For commercials, after being with Bill Cunningham for many years, I signed on with Vic Sutton, Dick Barth, and Rita Vennari, who were sub-agents at Cunningham's, when they left to form their own company. It was a good move, and I had many happy and successful years with SBV doing both on-camera and voice over work. Debbie Cope also was a big factor in my making inroads in the commercial field, and I cherish her friendship to this day.

I've been blessed that so many really good, nice people have helped me along the way.

COMMERCIALS & THE NO-LOOK LOOK

Thank God for commercials. They sure paid the bills - and well. My very first commercial was for Cadillac, especially made to be shown in color (WOW - NEW TECHNOLOGY!) when the car company was the sole sponsor of the Masters Golf Tournament in the late 60s. We shot it way up in Bel Aire on the palatial estate of millionaire hotel owner Conrad Hilton. I remember we had to stop shooting when Mr. H. drove up to enter his home in his own mile-long caddy, complete with chauffeur and footman. People actually seemed to bow as he walked in. I guess that kind of money talks - just ask his great-granddaughter, "Paris."

For a while I was really hot in commercials. Reid Miles, a director with whom I worked a lot at the time, said "Hank, you have the no-look look." Is that a Hollywoodism or what? Whatever, I seemed to land lots of good national spots in the 60s and 70s. One of the more prominent was for Hai Karate after-shave lotion. We shot it all day on the beach near Malibu. One reason I was cast was that I was so darn pale, puny, and un-lifeguard-like. Unfortunately, that almost did me in. After starting shooting at 8:00 A.M., by noon I already was getting pink from the sun, and by 6 P.M. I could give a lobster a run for his money. Man, did I get a burn. But at least I could enjoy every male's fantasy of having twenty beautiful bikini-clad blondes chasing me down the beach yelling, "Hey - what's that after-shave you're wearing?"

Another commercial I did that ran a lot was for Panasonic television. The thrust of the message was that the Panasonic picture was so real the images would come right out of the TV screen into your living room. The script had me watching a pirate movie in my easy chair at home. A colorful parrot, which was perched on a buccaneer's arm, then flew out of the TV and went straight to me. But that damn bird wanted more air-time: when the camera rolled the moment he landed on my shoulder, the foul fowl turned his head around, looked me in the eye, and proceeded to put his razor-sharp beak around my tender nose. He could have severed my schnoz! The bird's trainer was off-camera and scared as hell. I thought he would have apoplexy. But I didn't lose my cool and did a shocked reaction-take to the parrot until the director finally said "cut." Because of this unexpected event, they threw out the planned script and used the footage of the bird biting my nose in the final version of the commercial. Ever since then, I have an inordinate fear of wayward parrots.

I did several spots for McDonald's. On some, I often was their spokesman, a counter-boy talking directly into the camera. On others, I was like a male Rockette, dancing and singing in big Busby Berkeley-like production numbers directed by Howard Morris: "You deserve a break today, so get up and get away to McDonalds." Those required a week of rehearsal just to make them ready to shoot. The problem with doing a McDonald's commercial is that you sometimes had to eat the Big Macs, Egg MacMuffins, or MacFishes from morning to night and make them look appetizing on the screen. Believe me, after 50 or 60 MacFishes, it was necessary to have a barf-bag and a spittoon close by to help with the overflow. May I say "MacYuck!"

Sometimes landing a commercial brought more than I bargained for - like pain. In one TV spot, I was Maytag repairman Jesse White's assistant. Jesse had made a whole second career about being "lonely" on his job because Maytag appliances supposedly never broke down. One of the criteria at the audition was that the actor cast as his assistant had to be able to stand on his head because, as the script said, that would fight boredom. "Hell," I thought, "I can do that." So after three callbacks, I got the part. That was all well and good except for one nearly fatal problem: standing on your head, if you can do it, is a breeze - if it's only for a minute or two. However, standing on your head for an entire day's shooting is entirely another matter. I learned the very hard way that the human body when upside down from 9:00 A.M. until 5:00 P.M. squashes all one's organs against each other, creating, first discomfort and then progressing on to excruciating pain. I almost passed out doing that one. But when the residuals started coming in, all was forgiven and nearly forgotten, and I wasn't lonely or bored at all.

There were many more. I was a surprised father who needed "a piece of the rock" in the delivery room of the maternity ward for Prudential when triplets unexpectedly arrived. I played a sailor on leave trying to telephone my girl friend from the ship's dock for Pacific Bell, but getting Ann B.

Davis ("Alice" on "The Brady Bunch") on the line by mistake. Then I was an office worker giving my boss Lee J. Cobb static in a spot for Commercial Credit. I played Avery Schreiber's nemesis in a karate studio as I tried to take away his Doritos. I was a young executive who danced on top of my desk at the office with Judy Kaye and all the stenographers in a big musical production for Kentucky Fried Chicken. I did a series of spots for Crest Toothpaste as the son of country storeowner, "Mr. Goodwin." My dad was portrayed by Oscar-winner Arthur O'Connell; years later I ran into Arthur on the streets of Beverly Hills, but gradually realized that he had no idea where he was or even who he was - Alzheimer's disease had ravaged his once-brilliant mind since last we met. I portrayed a fumbling 18th century Casanova trying to woo a voluptuous courtesan with cheese spread in a parody of the sexy eating scene in the movie "Tom Jones." I was cast as an inept new car owner being patiently instructed by the voice of my old pal Casey Kasem in a GM - Mark Of Excellence ad. I did shtick as "Adam" wearing long-johns in the Garden of Eden to Deidre Hall's "Eve" in a commercial for some slop the Gallo Brothers produced called "Boone's Farm Apple Wine." On and on ...

I figured out one time that I had done about 500 commercials over the years. Many were "national spots" that were broadcast all over the USA and Canada. I used some commercials as auditions for roles in TV series and films, because, in a sense, they were little movies in themselves. That was just the point made by Dick Clark when he showcased one of my efforts on his NBC-TV "World's Greatest Commercials" hour. It was the first commercial ever made for the Honda Civic and was put together by groundbreaking ad-agency Chiat-Day. Son-of-a-gun if it didn't win some awards. In it, I run into a pretty young thing in a supermarket parking lot and am as impressed by her car as I am by her. "Wow," I say, "You have a really unique body design!" At the end of the spot, after extolling the virtues of both the Honda and the girl, I make my move by asking her, "Would you like to go with me to a Lithuanian Film Festival?," to which she replies, "Your car or mine?" It really was a one-minute movie - complete with a happy ending.

Voice-overs were fun to do also. These off-camera epics were highly sought-after as sometimes an actor could do several in a day. My friend Dick Noel carved his own niche as a v-o artist and jingle singer in Chicago and pretty much was the only game in the Windy City in that lucrative field. Dick sometimes would do 15-20 spots a day! I was happy to get one or two a week. The advantage of doing voice-overs for me was that my getting older didn't really matter: since the audience couldn't see me, I still could sound young and do teenage and young adult v-o roles into my forties and even fifties. The competition was fierce, however, as the residuals could be sensational: I once lost a voice-over to Paul Newman – why get Hank Jones when you could land Paul Newman to sell your product? You never knew who you'd be working with on a voice-over. One time I threw lines back and forth to Ted Cassidy ("Lurch" on "Addams Family") and Kenneth Mars (remember "Springtime For Hitler" in the original "Producers"?). What a combo!

Many fellow thespians that I would run into on interviews for commercials eventually hit much greater heights. I remember Harrison Ford often showing up for auditions in his grubby overalls, taking a break from his bill-paying job of being a carpenter. Cindy Williams, later "Shirley" on "Laverne & Shirley," played my girlfriend before her career took off, and she always was a blast to work with. Teri Garr, long before "Young Frankenstein" and "Tootsie," often auditioned with me, playing my wife. And I'll never forget good-guy Tom Hanks in the early stages of his acting days. Tom had recently arrived from Oakland, near where I grew up, and he sort of gravitated to me for tips on how to survive in his new Hollywood world. He practically was "in your face" like an eager puppy dog with all his questions. Tom especially was fascinated with what it was like to work on the older TV shows I did like "My Three Sons," as he had sort of grown up with those programs as a kid. I'm very happy that he's made it so big. As they say, it couldn't happen to a nicer guy.

IN COMMERCIALS, I WAS
THE GUY WITH THE "NO-LOOK-LOOK!"

THAT BLANKETY-BLANK PARROT WASN'T SUPPOSED TO BITE MY NOSE IN THIS NATIONAL PANASONIC COMMERCIAL. BUT - SURPRISE - HE SURE DID!

DEMO REELS FOR VOICE-OVER TAPES

"Three?" gasps the young father of triplets. "I need another piece of the Rock." Prudential's most popular new commercial underscores the basic need for life insurance . . . family protection.

EUE/SCREEN GEMS

MAY 19, 1972

DEAR HANK,

IN ADDITION TO WHAT I HOPE WILL BE A CLOSET FULL OF
RESIDUALS, LET ME ADD MY THANKS AND GRATITUDE FOR YOUR
COOPERATION, EFFORT AND TALENT. I CAN TELL YOU NOW THAT
WITH THE EXCEPTION OF YOUR CONTRIBUTION, SHOOTING THE
MCDONALD'S COMMERCIALS WAS THE MOST DIFFICULT DIRECTORIAL
ASSIGNMENT I HAVE EVER ENCOUNTERED. I WILL TREASURE THE
REMEMBERANCE OF YOUR GENEROUS UNDERSTANDING LONG AFTER
ALL THE AWARDS ARE COVERED WITH DUST.

FONDLY,

HOWARD MORRIS

HM/dm

Record them over and over again.
The life of a Scotch® brand cassette is a long one. Even when you record on it time after time after time.

Because there's a tough binder that keeps the magnetic coating from wearing off. So even after hundreds of replays or re-recordings, you get great sound quality.

We wish you a long and happy life. 'Cause you'll need it to keep up with your Scotch cassettes.

Play them back without jamming.
The life of a Scotch® brand cassette is a long one. Even when you play it time after time after time.

Because there's a Posi-Trak® backing that helps prevent jamming and reduces wow and flutter. And the cassette shell is made with a plastic that can withstand 150°F.

We wish you a long and happy life. 'Cause you'll need it to keep up with your Scotch cassettes.

Scotch® Cassettes.
They just might outlive you.

THIS PRINT AD RAN FULL-PAGE IN ROLLING STONE, TIME, & NEWSWEEK. THEY AGED ME DOWN TO 16 YEARS AND UP TO 80. IT TOOK NEARLY A WEEK TO SHOOT AT REID MILES STUDIOS

AMANDA JONES & HER AGED FATHER POSE
FOR A COMMERCIAL BROCHURE SHOT

READY WHEN YOU ARE, C.B.

So much of how an actor or performer comes across on the screen depends on the skill of the guy directing him. I've always been blessed in that most everyone who directed me in a film, TV show, or commercial was, not only extremely talented, but also easy to get along with.

Bill Burch was my first experience with the breed, directing most all the "Tennessee Ernie Ford Shows" on which Dean and I appeared. Bill was a tall, balding, husky, no-nonsense sort of guy, with a big bass voice that echoed all through the studio. Some of the crew later told me they were intimidated by him, but I never had any problem. He and several of his staff, including the wonderful Ginny Benjamin - his girl Friday upon whom he relied heavily, came from the old "Queen For A Day" program on ABC daytime television. They loved to regale us with the maudlin sob-stories told by contestants on that show who were all trying to be chosen the Queen in order to win a bevy of prizes: talk about black humor! Bill wasn't too imaginative with his choice of visual shots, however: many of our musical numbers were filmed in medium or even long shots, with close-ups at a minimum (maybe he was trying to tell us something?). Bill was gambling with two wet-behind-the-ears college kids on their first national television show, but after we settled in and kept learning and getting better, he seemed pleased with our performances (positive fan-mail from viewers and endorsements from Ernie's parents didn't hurt): after the first one-hundred shows we taped, Bill and Ernie sent a nice note about how pleased they were with us, which certainly brightened our day. After his wife died, Bill remarried to Vonnie King, one of the famous King Sisters of the big-band era, ran Universal Studios "industrial" film department for many years, and finally moved to Sacramento where he did a conservative talk-radio show until he retired and passed away in 2005.

My first director as an actor couldn't have been better one for a beginner like me: Gene Reynolds was a former kid actor ("Boys Town," the "Andy Hardy" series) who had great empathy for the pressure we were under to deliver a good performance. He was patient and made it easy. Gene later went on to be President of the Director's Guild of America and was the creator and producer of the wonderful "M.A.S.H." series on TV.

I remember some of the other directors with great affection too. Marc Daniels directed me in several TV commercials for Boone's Farm Wine. He was a real pioneer of early television ("I Love Lucy," "Kraft TV Theater," "Star Trek," and "Ben Casey") and could zip through a script like a surgeon, cutting it down to playable size. In Marc's spots as I mentioned before, I always played opposite Deidre Hall – Adam to her Eve in the Garden of Eden. Deidre was one of the most dedicated and ambitious actresses I ever worked with; Marc would have to pull her away from studying other scripts just to get her to concentrate on the job at hand. She always enlisted me to feed her the lines she had to memorize for her constant auditions for all the soap operas she was up for. Marc and I both should have known that Deidre would end up eventually as one of the major divas on daytime dramas, playing Marlena Evans on "Days Of Our Lives" for over thirty years.

I guess my favorite director in commercials was Howard Morris, a marvelous character actor who first came to fame (along with Carl Reiner) as Sid Caesar's sidekick on the old "Your Show of Shows" classic TV program. Howie was a blast to work with, full of energy, and always doing shtick to relieve the tension the suits from the ad agencies sometimes brought to the set. I did several big musical production commercials with him for MacDonald's and Kentucky Fried Chicken that required a week of rehearsal before we even started filming. They all had intricate choreography, and we became like "Rockettes" as we sang and danced our way into America's homes. I always tried to be bright and happy on the set, and Howie kept needling me to "cheer down, Hank!" Howie eventually went back into acting as a member of Mel Brook's stock company in his crazy movies like "High Anxiety" and wound up as the memorable Ernest T. Bass on the old "Andy Griffith Show." He died in 2005 and really left a void in the business with his passing. A great guy!

Richard Chambers was another former actor who directed me in several TV commercials. I once did a Blatz beer commercial for Richard where I was drinking the product at a bar. The guy who played the bartender didn't show up for the late-night filming at 3 AM, so Richard quickly called an old pal, character actor Vince Gardenia (Cher's put-upon father in "Moonstruck"), to come over immediately to the LA Skid Row establishment in which we were shooting to take the part. On the set, I happened to mention to Richard's girlfriend that I had a Boone's Farm Wine ad on the air at the time. Little did I know that beer and wine were sometimes considered "conflicts" for actors if they were being broadcast in the same locales. They telephoned my agent, Vic Sutton, in the middle of the night and woke him up to work things out with the two agencies. After much worry and apprehension on my part, they decided that Boone's Farm Wine was SO bad a product that Blatz didn't even consider it competition, so they let it slide. WHEW! For a while on that cold LA night, I thought I was going to be fired and then sued.

In films, I had several directors who stand out in my memory. Michael O'Herlihy, a wild Irishman with a wicked grin, led the team on several "Mr. Novak" TV shows I did at MGM and then was comfortable casting me in his Disney movie "The One And Only Genuine Original Family Band." Richard Fleischer, a clever man who had his plate full in directing the epic "Tora! Tora! Tora!, was patient and kind to me as I simulated flying over Pearl Harbor on December 7th, 1941. I did lots and lots of print work with Reid Miles for magazines like "Rolling Stone," "Time," "Newsweek," and even "Playboy." Some were Norman Rockwellish full-page ads that required actors, not models. Reid was a genuine piece of work, but could be cruel: he once greeted a young Asian actress at an audition for him with, "Well I've seen *weak links* before." Boris Sagal, as noted before, initially was interested in me for a large role in Elvis' "Girl Happy," but then, when that didn't pan out, still used me in a smaller part in that classic beach picture; sadly, after helming the memorable "Rich Man, Poor Man" miniseries, he met his death on location - decapitated by an out-of-control whirling helicopter blade.

The film director I worked the most for over the years was the distinguished Robert Stevenson at Disney. He was an Englishman, very proper and somewhat reserved, but with a noticeable twinkle in his eye. Robert worked almost always from illustrated storyboards made in conjunction with the Disney sketch artists that detailed each and every shot he would eventually make. He liked using me, because, as he laughingly said, "nobody played a goofy kid any better." Robert made some great movies over the years, starting out with "Tom Brown's School Days" in Britain and then writing the screenplay and directing the formidable Orson Welles as the brooding Rochester in "Jane Eyre." Working with Bill Walsh as producer, Robert directed "Old Yeller," "Kidnapped," "That Darn Cat," and the immortal "Mary Poppins" at Walt's studio; Robert was my director in "Blackbeard's Ghost," "Herbie Rides Again," and "Shaggy D.A." He always let me come up with my own pieces of business for the Disney characters I portrayed and would quietly chuckle off-camera as I tried to pull them off on screen. Robert gave me lots of rope to work with and seemed pleased with the results. When he died in 1986, the Disney organization forgot to put their usual full-page obituary ad in *Variety* honoring this important man who had done so much for the studio. So I wrote to the President/CEO of Disney Michael Eisner to complain about the oversight. Michael wrote me back the nicest letter, apologizing for the omission and agreeing that Disney Studio's unparalleled successes owed much to the marvelous talents of Robert Stevenson. He truly added his own special "spoonful of sugar" to make the medicine of the many films he directed go down so smoothly.

Bill Walsh, almost joined at the hip with Robert, actually was the most important man at the studio after Walt's passing. It was his job to carry on the Disney tradition and do what Walt would have wanted. On a "Merv Griffin TV Show" one time, using my track sequence at the finale of "Blackbeard's Ghost" as an example, Bill compared his producing job to being a chef in a fine restaurant, "getting all the best ingredients for the bouillabaisse, then carefully mixing them all together well for the final tasty dish to come out of the kitchen." He was so nice to me: I once was having dinner with my old friends Brenda and Russell White at Hamburger Hamlet in the Valley. We were at a booth, laughing and enjoying our meal, when I noticed Bill sitting alone and looking kind of sad at the counter (He recently had left his wife for a younger starlet-type, and I think was already regretting the move). He came over to our table and made me feel like a million bucks, telling my friends, "In 'Herbie Rides Again,' we had to give Hank *two* parts to play ('Sir Lancelot' and 'The surfer who rides the waves with Herbie'), just to ensure the movie would be a big hit." Not true, of course, but what a super-kind thing to say.

I tried to improve my craft as I went along. Sometimes it was quite a struggle, because I really felt more at home in the music world, where I started, than in the acting realm, where I ended up. I studied with the "voice-shrink" Marice Tobias for a while; she emphasized the psychological approach to the advertising copy we were given to read, as well as an in-depth look at why we were in the business to begin with - very helpful! Then I took several voice-over workshops with Bill Bell, engineer-owner of Bell Sound Studios in Hollywood. Bill was a tough taskmaster who got us pros to really stretch ourselves into areas where we probably wouldn't have gone. Guest lecturers like Tim MacIntire, Danny Dark, and my old Monopoly competitor Casey Kasem gave us hints and pointers. The Bell workshop really did help me, and I made a good supplemental living from voice-work for years – also thanks to good agents in my corner like Debbie Cope and Rita Vennari.

Another class I took was a cold-reading workshop at the Lee Strasberg Institute in Hollywood. One of the instructors was Burgess Meredith, that marvelous character actor in "Of Mice And Men," all the "Rocky" movies, and countless other memorable roles. One night Mr. Meredith (I never did feel comfortable enough to call him "Buzz," his nickname) said "in order to succeed, we had to want to be actors more than anything else in the world!" He asked everyone who felt that way to raise their hand. Everyone in the entire class nodded in agreement, applauded, and said, "Oh, yes - yes!" - except me. I sheepishly had to admit to myself that I just didn't have the drive and ambition that the others did. I thought that there *had* to be more to life than just TV and movies. I think my unconscious was telling me that I wasn't destined to be an actor forever.

Joe Bernard, a well-known familiar-faced character actor, was the other teacher in the class. I certainly was more a performer than a Method actor, but I stuck it out and did my best to fit in with all the Strasbergites. I came away with excellent hints on how to grasp hidden beats in difficult scripts, search out the inner life of the character I was portraying, and nail parts at auditions that otherwise might have gone to others. Joe Bernard had quite a story himself. He was a husky ethnic type with a big mustache and had started out in the business as Dustin Hoffman's roommate, starving with him in a cold-water flat in New York in the earliest years of their careers. But as time went on and the years rolled by, they lost touch with each other. Then one day Joe was visiting the Paramount lot in Hollywood. He heard that Hoffman was shooting a film on a nearby soundstage and decided to look him up. As Joe tells it, he walked in the stage door, and there in a far corner sitting on a high-backed director's chair was his old roommate, Dustin Hoffman. Dustin was surrounded by people fussing over him, touching up his makeup, and fixing his hair - all answering to his beck and call and every whim. Beautiful starlets were everywhere, looking up adoringly at him with big eyes and welcoming smiles. Out of the corner of his eye Hoffman saw Joe Bernard shyly walking towards him, recognized him, and then yelled out in loud voice for all to hear, "HEY JOE BERNARD - LOOK WHAT HAPPENED TO *ME*!!"

I was lucky to work a lot; but also, in the course of my career, I often would meet with some big-name directors for a role, but then - sad to say - wouldn't land the part. Sometimes the meetings would be actors' "cattle calls": dehumanizing lineups where all of us would stand in a row while the producer or director eyed and evaluated us carefully, looking us over like we were pieces of meat. I remember Sam Spiegel doing this to Paul Williams, Richard Dreyfuss, and me (and about thirty other young thespians) as we all tried out for a small role in 1966's "The Chase" at Columbia, starring Marlon Brando. Spiegel (known in his earlier days as "S. P. "Eagle") was a big-leaguer, who had produced such classics as "On The Waterfront," "The African Queen," and "Lawrence Of Arabia." Spiegel strode up and down in front of us like a martinet in his fur-lined topcoat, scowling and whispering secret asides to his underlings. No talent was involved, it seemed, in his eventual decision: just our "look." For a guy like me who supposedly had "the no-look look," this seemed like a losing game - and it was.

A meeting with "the ultimate Hun" Otto Preminger was met with equal trepidation. Otto, I was told, was two people. He could be suave and charming (he had a reputation as quite a ladies' man, fathering a child with Gypsy Rose Lee and having affairs with many actresses in town including Dorothy Dandridge); but he also played "Mr. Freeze" on TV's "Batman," and it was said often lived up to that character's name. Preminger had had a long string of acting roles playing Nazi sadists and as a director was known for his screaming tantrums and sadistic behavior towards his cast and crew. So I really didn't know what to expect when I arrived for an interview with him for a role in his forthcoming film "Hurry Sundown," starring Jane Fonda.

I walked into his well-appointed office at Paramount Studios, and there he was sitting behind a huge desk. Otto Preminger was nattily dressed in a sports jacket with a stylish scarf around his bulky neck. His bald dome seemed to shine under the fanlight whirling slowly above his head. He was reserved and polite, but shortly after the meeting began I'm afraid my own preconceived image of the man began to take over. My growing discomfort led to wild imaginings. I remember thinking I'd never seen anyone look this intimidating before: I began to feel that he was the leopard, and I was the prey. Blessed hindsight now tells me that this was all in my head, but at the time I was scared as hell. So, in a moment of quiet panic to hopefully lighten up the interview, I tried to be bright and cheery, telling jokes and rambling on about this and that. WRONG! The more I nattered and chattered, the more he glowered and frowned. My agent Jack Gilardi of GAC was just withering away in his corner chair, hoping that I'd shut up. He knew that I wasn't making any points with Mr. P. and undoubtedly was hoping that my ridiculous behavior wasn't rubbing off on Otto's opinion of him. Finally, imagining that my own personal safety was somehow in jeopardy, I muttered a hurried "goodbye," headed for what I thought was the front door, and walked directly into Preminger's personal wardrobe closet. I found myself surrounded by a collection of suits, jackets, pants, and scarves - smothering in a Teutonic, sartorial prison. I finally bumbled my way to the real office door and escaped. But I swear I could almost feel the death-ray look emanating from Otto Preminger's eyes following me as I scurried off the Paramount lot.

But most directors were just the opposite.. Robert Wise, who started as editor on "Citizen Kane" and then helmed everything from "The Day The Earth Stood Still" to "West Side Story" to "Sound of Music" made me feel welcome and wanted when I auditioned for a part of a young German crewman in his "The Hindenburg" picture (he didn't want me enough to give me the part, however). Norman Jewison was an old friend and fan of Ernie Ford, so we had a lot to talk about when I was up for a role in his "The Russians Are Coming - The Russians Are Coming!" Peter Bogdanovich gave me much of his time when I met him for a role in "The Last Picture Show." He was young and brash and relished talking about his friendship with "Orson." I remember asking him, "Orson *who*?," which he didn't think was funny. I really turned him on, however, when I mentioned *my* friendship with Stan Laurel. Peter then picked my brain about Stan and borrowed my own personal 16mm prints of some L&H movies to use in preparation for his own comedy, "What's Up Doc?" Even though I hired the amazing Robert Easton to coach me in the subtle dialect spoken by residents portrayed in the picture (I asked Robert to teach me a Texas accent, and he said, "which county?"), I didn't land that part in "Last Picture Show" either. Actually, I was the one who put the brakes on first in that particular decision: I felt the language in the script was pretty raunchy, and that, if I got the job, I would never work at Disney again. Who knew that flick would get an Oscar? I could have been the new Cybill Shepherd!

Along these lines of "close, but no cigar," I recall the crazy try-out I had for 20th Century Fox's humungous musical "Hello Dolly," starring Barbra Streisand. I was up for the major role of "Barnaby (to be played alongside Michael Crawford's "Cornelius"). The part was very similar to all the other characters I'd been doing on TV and at Disney. Because of this, I had moved up the Barnaby ladder of consideration quickly, and now it was finally time to meet the director of the film, the legendary actor/dancer Gene Kelly.

I arrived at the studio for my appointment in a huge sound stage that looked like an airplane hanger, eager to meet one of my long-time idols. As I walked in the door, a rather short husky man who was as bald as Elmer Fudd came up to me. He said, "Hi Hank - I'm Gene Kelly. Can you dance?" Startled at his crome-dome appearance and trying to cover my surprise, I blurted back, "Of course I can dance!," trying to forget that it took two long weeks of intensive choreographic training to teach me years before in Disney's "Family Band. I tried to follow the simple steps Mr. K. was giving me to do, but immediately proved that I had two left feet and certainly was *no* Gene Kelly. I think he really felt that acting-wise I was perfect for the part, because he looked so sad and disappointed that I couldn't cut the dance moves. But he was kind in his goodbye - giving me a wave and a "sorry, kid" that sent me out the door. Whatta' loss – forget Cybill Shepherd - I could have been the new Fred Astaire: so what if I needed about fifty years more training.

MEET ME AT MUSSO'S

I've always liked good restaurants, and Hollywood and environs was chock full of them. My mouth waters just remembering the good ones where I spent many happy hours: savoring the juicy prime rib, Yorkshire pudding, and creamed spinach at "Lawrey's" on LaCienega; ogling the platter of steaks from which to choose before the meal at Edna Earl's "Fogcutter" on La Brea; watching the flow of a real waterfall with a thunderous storm above it every fifteen minutes inside "The Islander" in Beverly Hills; and trying my first taste of roast boar at the Blue Boar" below the Sunset Strip. There were so many others: the best Chinese restaurant ever downtown with the unlikely name of "Man Fook Lo;" old classics like Chasen's and Perino's still attracting the old guard like Mae West and Alfred Hitchcock; Italian *trattorias* like Dino's and Villa Capri that probably had connections with 'da boys; down-home casuals like "The Shack" on Cole and "Tick Tock" on Vine Street; and ethnic winners like Nate & Al's, Jerry's Deli, Art's Deli, and Kantor's on Fairfax.

I once had a boisterous lunch with a group of comedy writers at Kantor's. They all happened to be Jewish, except me. The hard-boiled waitress took all their orders quickly giving no lip or aggravation to any of them, but when she got to me she raised her eyebrows like I didn't belong at the table and asked me, "And what do *you* want?" I guess I was the token "goy," standing out from the others. I was temped to order "corned beef on white with mayonnaise," but fearing for my life, I didn't.

Sometimes it was difficult not to eavesdrop listening to conversation at a neighboring table. I was dining at Harry's Bar & Grill in Century City one evening, seated next to the table occupied by famous Washington D.C. columnist Jack Anderson. He was telling his friends a wonderful story about President Harry Truman:

> Mr. Anderson was taking a shortcut to get to work, briskly walking across the mall in front of the Washington monument. As he was passing in front of one of the government buildings, he noticed an old mustached gentleman hobbling along with a cane, wearing a somewhat-shabby

dark suit and derby hat. His appearance and demeanor suggested that he was probably a retired military officer who had seen better days. At that very moment, along came a motorcade with a limousine taking President Truman back to the White House after a state dinner. As the motorcade passed the elderly man, the old gentleman took off his hat, held it over his heart, and stood at attention as a sign of respect for the Presidency. The convoy continued on until, as Jack Anderson said, the car carrying Truman stopped abruptly ten feet beyond with a sudden screeching of brakes. The limousine then backed up abruptly and halted right in front of the old man. Out of the car popped President Harry S. Truman. He walked directly to the old soldier and firmly shook his hand. Mr. Anderson said he heard President Truman simply say the words, "Thank you, sir - thank you *very* much." With that, the President of the United States returned to the motorcade, got in his limousine, and resumed his trip back to the White House.

Jack Anderson told his dinner companions at the next table that it was one of the most moving scenes he ever witnessed.

The people-watching at some of these eateries was as much an attraction as the food. I remember ...

Being amazed that the maitre d' at "Tail of the Cock" in the Valley was former cowboy movie star Johnny Mack Brown ...

Sitting in the adjoining booth next to 300-pound "Cannon" actor William Conrad and watching him order and then completely devour *two* entrees and *two* sets of soups, salads, and desserts there in one sitting ...

Staring wide-eyed as Jack Nicholson and Anjelica Huston waltzed out of "The Luau" in Beverly Hills wearing their matching shades and white tailored outfits to applause from the other diners ...

Joining in singing "Happy Birthday" to 30s dancing star Ruby Keeler at a French restaurant in Toluca Lake and hoping she would segue into a chorus of "I Want To Be Happy," "42nd Street," or "Broadway Melody" ...

Hearing American Indian actor Iron Eyes Cody confidently order saurbrauten, spaetzle and a fine wine at "Little Vienna" in North Hollywood, completely blowing his Native-American image ...

Watching a wasted Brian Jones of the Rolling Stones looking jaded and bored at a hip spot on the Sunset Strip, not knowing he'd soon be found floating dead in a swimming pool in just a few months time ...

Quietly laughing as Steve Allen spoke constantly into his portable tape recorder making verbal notes for his next book at "Aux Delices" in Sherman Oaks while his wife Jayne Meadows had only herself to talk to all through dinner ...

Feeling badly for Michael Caine, recently arrived from England, eating all alone in a booth at Universal City and looking forlorn and homesick ...

Going to a fabulous Writer's Guild "Blood Drive" luncheon at Scandia with my friend Paul Pumpian, and then nearly fainting afterwards giving blood while next to me swashbuckling actor Cornel Wilde did his macho act and came through the same ordeal just fine ...

Thrilled when our manager George Burke introduced Dean and me as "a couple of up and comers" to his friend the classy Nat "King" Cole when the velvet-voiced singer stopped by our table to visit during a Brown Derby lunch ...

And feeling jittery and nervous sitting opposite "Old Blue Eyes" Frank Sinatra at Martoni's in Hollywood every time his buddy and bodyguard Jilly Rizzo readjusted his shoulderholster.

Wild times!

But since the 1960s, my home away from home in Hollywood has been Musso & Frank's Grill. "Meet me at Musso's" has been a byword for myself and countless other starving souls in the entertainment industry since it opened its doors at 6667 Hollywood Boulevard way back in 1919. With its ancient wallpaper, subdued lighting, and mahogany booths, its patrons are whisked back to another time - perhaps a better time - when good food and good conversation were inseparable. Charlie Chaplin's studio was nearby, and he ate almost every lunch there holding court in his own booth. Stars like Bogart and Monroe, and writers such as Dashiell Hammett, William Faulkner, F. Scott Fitzgerald, Raymond Chandler, and Ernest Hemingway all knew Musso's well.

I liked to eat at the counter. In that way I could watch the steaks and chops charcoal-broiled on the grill right in front of me. The smell of that meat wafted through the whole restaurant and made a direct line through our collective noses down to our tastebuds. The regulars at the counter became a family. Nelson Riddle, Sinatra and Nat Cole's genius arranger, was there two or three times a week at lunch, and I so enjoyed my conversations with this man so instrumental in making the music I loved. Gilligan's buddy "The Captain" Alan Hale Jr. and his charming wife were frequent habitués at our long table, and he sometimes even wore his Captain's hat pulled back on his head while he enjoyed Musso's famous flannel cakes.

You never knew who would get on a stool beside you at the counter. I shared a meal with health-guru Jack LaLanne there one time, reminding him that my Dad's real estate office in Oakland was just across the street from his very first health studio and that my cousin Harrison Bedell had once written comedy lines for him (Jack remembered Harrison well and with great affection, which made me very happy). I recall trying to keep my eyes on my chicken potpie when Russ Meyer would bring in one of his busty starlets from his soft-core films and treat her to lobster thermidor. One rainy evening I enjoyed my lamb chops while sharing conversations with Miss America Emcee Bert Parks to my left and Will Rogers Junior sitting on my right as Sean Penn and Madonna strolled by us heading for a booth. FUN!

I had a big problem there one morning. I was driving into have flannel cakes at the counter for a late breakfast and heard on the radio that Bing Crosby had just died on a golf-course in Spain. I was heartsick. Bing used to record in his later years at Valentine's Studios in North Hollywood where I did too. He was so "normal." Jimmy Valentine would often find Der Bingle seated on the studio's front porch, reading the LA Times, and smoking his pipe while waiting for the session to start. People would drive by and do double-takes at seeing The Old Groaner just relaxing there for all the world to see. When I went inside Musso's that morning after hearing the sad news, who should I see at the counter but Bing Crosby's best friend and golfing buddy, Phil Harris having his first Bloody Mary of the day. My quandary was whether to go up to Phil and tell him the sad news. I really didn't know how the blow would hit him, so, after much thought, decided "who am I to go up to someone and relay such tragic news?" I didn't, and Phil and remained at the counter drinking and eating for a couple of hours until he went out to the parking lot, undoubtedly to hear of Bing's passing from someone else.

The clientele at Musso's was eclectic to say the least. Wealthy society ladies would dine there while their chauffeurs waited in the parking lot keeping their Rolls Royces warm for them. Celebrities would arrive in their tuxedos and long dresses to enjoy a meal prior to attending an awards ceremony and be seated in an adjoining booth to a punk rocker with long hair, tattoos, and piercings showing from every visible orifice. I especially loved sitting next to the bookies and racetrack touts at the counter, listening to their Damon Runyonese excuses as to why their particular horse came in last and sharing inside dope on future races. An occasional hood often could be viewed near the door, ready to make a quick exit if the law happened by. Star-wanna--bees hung out, carefully budgeting their menu choices, hoping to be discovered by a cigar-smoking producer or talent scout. Pure eccentrics were patrons too, like the guy sitting next to me one time who took out his false teeth and put them in his water glass prior to eating his chicken-okra soup. It was an intriguing mix.

I got to know the waiters and cooks who served at the counter well. There was Nick The Cook who always put secret spices on his meats for his regulars, so that when you bit into "steak a/la Nick" you knew you were eating something super special (and man did that garlic ever linger). Nick was a New York tough guy, but he had a soft spot too that he would reveal sometimes when he'd had a bit too much to drink before coming on duty at the counter. Nick lost his wife in the early part of his Musso's years, and I don't think he ever recovered from the blow. He eventually left the establishment and sort of drifted off into a sad and lonely haze. Charlie was another chef, and he worked during the daytime hours. He would make up special crepes for me (at no charge), filled with fruit or even crab, just to see if I liked them. I sure did! There were so many others there that brightened my days and nights: waiters like Eppie, Paul, and especially Raoul; busboys like Nacho and Jerry; office staff like the wonderful Ricky; maitre d's like Jesse; and the unobtrusive Mrs. Keegle who was the daughter of the original family that owned Musso's at the start. She never liked the limelight and stayed back in the kitchen making sure everything ran smoothly, and that the quality of service and food remained tip-top.

The waiters at Musso's were known for being a bit gruff and brusque in the main dining room; but those at the counter were quite the opposite. Wilbert was a short somewhat-bald little man who worked for years behind the counter. He could carry huge trays of food and balance them with the skill of a circus performer. One night, he caught the edge of one of the trays filled with food on a protective plastic partition in front of the fireplace, and the whole collection of steaks, fish, vegetables, and sauces came crashing down on me sitting on my stool opposite the fire. I was covered in bearnaise, bordelaise, hollandaise, salmon, chicken potpie, and sand dabs. Poor Wilbert was so embarrassed - this had never happened to him before. Musso's gave me my dinner for free and paid for the cleaner's bill. At least it gave me a chance to sample some of the dishes I hadn't tried yet.

Wilbert had a sad end. He was on his way to the restaurant for work one afternoon and stopped at a local convenience store for an item he needed. As he arrived and was heading for the one available parking place in the small lot, another car darted in front of him and grabbed the spot Wilbert wanted. A heated argument started between Wilbert and the pushy driver, resulting out of the blue in Wilbert being shot dead - fighting over a lousy parking place for heaven's sake. His memorial service drew all of the Musso's staff and many of his devoted customers. The Alan Hales were there, Nelson Riddle too, and out of the corner of my eye I saw Buddy Ebsen saying his rosary with tears in his eyes. Wilbert left a big vacuum at the Musso's counter with his passing.

But my main man at the counter then and now has been my favorite waiter and dear friend, Manuel Felix. Manny was born in Mexico in 1937 and grew up in Arizona. He worked first at the Ambassador Hotel in downtown in L.A., then Hollywood's Villa Capri, and finally moved on to Musso's where he has become almost an institution. You can't miss Manny Felix: he wears both a silver cat on his scarlet jacket denoting his feline surname as well as a constant smile. My daughter Amanda has been coming to see him at the counter ever since she was two years old and, along with her Dad, always looks forward to our visits.

Manny is an entertainer along with a being a super waiter. He sings as he serves and probably knows more obscure songs from the 40s and 50s than anyone I know. I was sitting next to renowned jazz singer Anita O'Day one afternoon at Musso's, and she was jivin' and laughin' at Manny's show along with everyone else within earshot. He might make one of his patented caesar salads for you, twirling the plate on one finger prior to serving, and then immediately launch into his unique version of "Sh-Boom" before bringing on your short ribs. But what really continues to wow us all who come to see Manny along with the food is his tremendous ability at performing the dying art of slight-of-hand magic right in front of our noses. He can make coins appear and disappear at will and pour salt out of the palm of his seemingly-empty hand like a modern-day Houdini.

Manny's greatest gift, however, is in making the customer feel like "family." Through highs and lows of my personal and professional life, Manny and Musso's always made me feel welcome and accepted. Without going into personal details, Manny has had some pretty big bumps in his own road of life, but uses them as "lessons learned" to be shared with others. Never preachy, always caring, he's probably one of the most spiritual souls I've met in my life. The owners at Musso's use Manny Felix a lot in public relations for the restaurant, and they couldn't have made a better choice.

MORE TINSELTOWN FOLLIES

Once I married Lori, we would entertain in our own home in North Hollywood and later Toluca Lake. In North Hollywood at our house at 4444 Simpson Avenue, we had some eclectic gatherings. At one dinner, my friend Sammy Jackson brought his then-flame June Wilkinson as his date. She was one of the first Playboy Playmates and was stunning to say the least. But June had a particular problem at the dinner table: her breasts were so large she had to rest them on the table in between courses - I kid you not! Sammy had lots of fun with her and took pride in the 8X10 glossy of June he had framed on his bed-stand which said, "To Sammy - Love & Hot Milk, June."

On another occasion, one of our guests was Jeanne Cagney, sister of Jimmy, brought to dinner by my Ford Show pal, Ginny Benjamin. Jeanne was a sweet gal and patiently answered all our questions about what it was like to grow up with her legendary sibling and appear with him, even playing his sister in "Yankee Doodle Dandy." Matty Matlock, that fabulous clarinetist on many Bing and Bob Crosby records, lived just across the street from us on Simpson Avenue, and we would often get together to gab about music, where it had been and where it was going. Another time later on when we had moved to Toluca Lake, Laurel & Hardy's favorite leading lady from the silents and early talkies Anita Garvin graced our table. I remember one evening in particular because that was the night Anita arrived yelling, "They've shot the Pope ... They've shot the Pope." As she was a strong Catholic, you could see how this horrified she was about this terrible event. Coincidentally just a few months before, I was watering the yard in Toluca Lake when who should fly directly over me in his helicopter but a visiting John Paul II on his way to a saying a big mass in Los Angeles. I went out in the street all by myself and waved at the Man In White high above. Son-of-a-gun if he didn't wave right back and give me a private blessing as I stood there looking up in the middle of Placidia Avenue. It almost made me become the first Methodist to enter the priesthood - but not quite.

David Foster, one of the town's top record producers, was father to Amanda's school chum, Amy. David has produced more major hit records than anyone I've ever heard of: classics for Barbara Streisand, Celine Dionne, Dolly Parton, Josh Groban, Whitney Houston, Michael Bublé, on and on. When he would join us at our home for dinner with his then-wife B.J., David loved to hear about my stone-age recording experiences on four track sessions at RCA. I think he felt as if Thomas Edison himself must have been my A&R man. I remember one special evening when I told David I had just seen Arthur Fiedler and the Boston Pops play a concert version of a hit song he wrote for the group Chicago called "After The Love Has Gone." He couldn't believe it, and was absolutely thrilled. Years later, Bonnie and I ran into him and his current wife Linda Thompson, formerly Elvis's girlfriend for many years, at Le Dome. David is still the good guy he always was, even with all the success. Nice guys DO finish first sometimes.

Lori and I put on a Christmas caroling party every year for our pals and serenaded round both neighborhoods. Toluca Lake had some nice big homes, and it was fun to try to sneak a peek inside some of them while singing "Deck The Halls" with Jan & Vickie Williams, Jerry and Jewel Jaffe Rannow, Eddie and Tanya Applegate, Jim and Judy Begg, Flo and Pete Renoudet, Bernadette Withers Cook, Candy and John Terry Bell, Lou Wagner, and the inimitable John Craig among others. Near our home Andy Griffith lived around the corner on Camarillo, Ken Berry resided up the street on Cahuenga, and Ronnie Howard's family had their digs a few blocks away - so we could say we sort of lived in "Mayberry *West*," I guess. Toluca Lake was home to Bob Hope's sprawling house and earlier Bing Crosby resided there too. The actual lake itself was notable for the times W. C. Fields would be out rowing, feeling no pain and three sheets to the wind, all the while trying to shoot swans out of the water with his BBgun.

As the years went by, I started getting recognized myself but usually not by name. Due to my work in sit-coms, Disney films, and especially my commercials, people would stare at me a lot, but never were quite sure from where they knew me. It was always, "Aren't you Joe's brother-in-law" or something like that (remember, I had what they said was "the no-look look"). I'm embarrassed to say that I took great delight in being this so-called familiar face. During the "Ernie Ford Show" years, if I would be out driving, I sometimes would go to a furniture store about the time the program aired and actually stand next to a TV set broadcasting the show until someone recognized me! How's that for early ego? I was a true legend in my own mind. But one day I got my comeuppance at Disneyland for this foolishness: my pal Larry Ray and I were waiting in line to get on the Matterhorn ride. "Blackbeard's Ghost" was just out at the time, and I had been signing a few autographs for people who had seen the movie. A young teenage girl behind me came up with what looked to be a pencil and pad in her hand. As I feigned a modest "Oh I'd be happy to ... " ready to sign my signature, all she said was "Would you mind moving? You're holding up the line." 'Nuff said - "Bang-Bang - She Shot Me Down!"

But oh, it was tough sometimes. The feast or famine aspects of being in the entertainment business are difficult to fully express to a "civilian." When an actor gets a job, it's terrific: but then when the production is completed comes the feeling that you'll never work again. The insecurity is rampant and insidious. For a while when Screen Actor's Guild decided to let their insurance cover all psychiatric doctor's visits for their members, they almost went broke, because as one union official put it distinctly, "All actors are crazy." That full Union coverage lasted only a few months before they had to pull it.

There was a whole group of guys who hung out together and had to go through this: besides my close "Caroling Party" pals mentioned before, there were James Cromwell, Archie Hahn, Jim Beach, Allan Hunt, Bob Moloney, Jed Allan, Gordon Metcaffe, Henry Gibson, Anson Williams, Alan Haufrect, Roy Stuart, George Winters, and a hundred others. When my friend Jerry Rannow wrote his excellent book *Surviving Hollywood* and asked me for my input, my sage advice was, "When you get your first TV series, don't go buy your boat too soon." And is that ever true.

And then there were the parts that got away. Besides being up for "Barnaby" in "Hello Dolly" and "Gopher" on "Love Boat," and any number of roles in "Last Picture Show" as previously mentioned, I was in consideration for "Harold" in "Harold & Maude," "Benjamin" in "The Graduate," the young NAZI who sings "You Are Sixteen Going On Seventeen" in "Sound of Music," and even the possibility of being one of "The Monkees" on TV. But hey – that's show-biz! Those roles just weren't meant to be – and every one of my friends noted above would have their variation of the same story.

We all kept as busy as we could. Some had other jobs to help pay the bills. Others had hobbies that took over our lives "in between pictures." I always said that all my genealogical activities were my therapy to get me through the slow times when the phone didn't ring (Many have risen to say, "The therapy didn't work, did it?"). We'd go to Screen Actors Guild meetings to commune with the few who were working or the many more who weren't (Someone once said that on any one given day over 98% of the Screen Actors Guild is unemployed). The SAG meeting gave us the opportunity to rub elbows with our officers like Charlton Heston and Walter Pidgeon and be uplifted by old SAG war-horses like Edward G. Robinson and Leon Ames. Then we'd bother our managers, agents, public relations people – anyone who could help us get work. We'd figure out ways to bug our casting-director friends like Virginia Martindale, Jim Lister, Sheila Manning, Lynn Stahlmaster, Hoyt Bowers, Trudy Booth, and Maxine Anderson. These good folks were largely sympathetic to us all, knowing that basically what was wrong was that there were too few parts for too many good, qualified actors; and if they were hiring lamb chops that day and you happened to be a pork chop, you could be the "Laurence Olivier of pork chops" – but you still wouldn't get the job.

Hollywood often doesn't have a memory. I was at a casting call for a commercial in the 70s and also there was the remarkable character actor Ian Wolfe. He's another thespian whose face you'd know in a second, but might not be familiar with his name. Mr. Wolfe had important roles in such classics as "Mutiny On The Bounty" and "Witness For The Prosecution" with Charles Laughton, "Rebel Without A Cause," "Seven Brides For Seven Brothers," "Mrs. Miniver," "Johnny Belinda," "You Can't Take It With You," "The Barretts Of Wimpole Street," *ad infinitum*. I stress all these credits because Ian Wolfe then was virtually a living walking, talking history lesson on the movies. By the time of the audition he was in his late 80s (he would live to be 96 – still acting when he died) and possessed a dignified and distinguished demeanor. We both were called in for the interview together to meet with the young twentyish director. He looked us over somewhat smugly and then asked Ian Wolfe, "Have you ever acted before? What have you done?" I wanted to slug the guy in the chops, but Mr. Wolfe responded with class: "Oh, I've been around a while. I made my first film in the early 30s and have worked steadily ever since." The director then buried his head in a magazine as the veteran actor reeled off his major credits. The director finally looked up and said curtly, "OK. Thank you. NEXT." How soon they forget.

Ageism, especially today, is a sad and prominent feature of the contemporary Hollywood scene. I have several friends who are members of the Writers Guild of America with years of experience and many film credits who now have to use false names to get in the studio doors. New studio owners (mostly corporate types who care more about the bottom line than the creative aspects) think only writers in their 20s can write material that will sell to the younger demographic audience. It sure is their loss.

As Stan Laurel once wrote me after I had just finished my first movie, "Sorry business is slow. It always is that way isn't it BETWEEN PICTURES?" Well, I was to quickly learn what it was like to be "between pictures" a lot. I was in the North Hollywood Unemployment Office one day filling out a form. Over the loudspeaker came a loud, intrusive voice that repeated: "Dana Andrews – go to the Disputed Claims Window … Dana Andrews - go to the Disputed Claims Window." A sad-faced, worn-looking man plodded his way to where he was supposed to go. It was the star of "Best Years Of Our Lives," "State Fair," and other major films, Dana Andrews. He was formerly President of the Screen Actors Guild, and here he was in the Unemployment Office fighting for a few extra bucks from the State. I'd known he'd had problems with alcohol abuse in the past, and life hadn't been easy for him. My heart went out to him. What he was going through could happen to any of us.

However, it wasn't always bad and sad. There were some character actors who did have a long, steady, and productive career. My goal was to work as much and last as long as my friend, Percy Helton, one of the most familiar faces and voices in Hollywood pictures. Percy and his wife Edna were introduced to me in the late 60s by their close friends Jerry Rannow and Jewel Jaffe. The Heltons sort of adopted the Rannows and vice-versa, and they were included in many of our parties and gatherings. What a life he led! Percy started in his father's vaudeville act and did some early silent pictures. After the legendary David Belasco cast him in some of his productions, George M. Cohan then took him under his wing and used him a number of his plays. Percy was a diminutive, sweet guy, with a high-pitched hoarse voice and breathy delivery that sounded like sandpaper on glass. With his immense and distinctive talent, Percy made small roles big. It was his brief but memorable appearance as a drunken Santa Claus in 1947's "Miracle On 34th Street" that really launched his career. He could do no wrong in featured roles such as "Sweetface" in "Butch Cassidy & The Sundance Kid," "Sam Brewster" in "Jailhouse Rock," "The Train-Conductor" in "The Music Man" ("River City – next station stop, River City," he announced), and classics like "A Star Is Born," "20,000 Leagues Under The Sea," "White Christmas," and a zillion TV shows. When I married Lori in 1968, my visiting Bay Area cousins were more excited about seeing Percy at the wedding than anyone else. I don't blame them.

Still with all the trials and guff we went through, it was never dull. Every day was an adventure. I never knew just who I'd run into. Among my fond people memories from my Hollywood "daze" ...

Having a chance to spend time alone laughing with Jack Benny, when he and I both showed up an hour too early for an industry banquet ...

Driving to work at the studios through Beverly Hills and seeing Cary Grant pick up his daughter from grade school in a car-pool like any normal parent would; and chuckling as Jimmy Stewart wrestled with two huge Irish setters on leashes who evidently thought they would try and walk *him* around the neighborhood ...

Being with Casey Kasem at a Beverly Hills fund-raiser filled with "fat-cats" who'd seen it all, but noting how all eyes turned when a surprisingly tiny Mae West sashayed in, flanked by two beefy muscle-men ...

Not recognizing the stunning Natalie Wood in my dentist's office, and, knowing she looked familiar and that I'd seen her someplace before, asking if she had once worked as an extra on *My Three Sons* ...

Worrying that I'd never get the smell of marijuana out of my clothes after walking by the open door of Sammy Davis Jr.'s hotel suite prior to a dinner we both attended ...

Following the diminutive 4'11" Judy Garland carrying her own wardrobe on hangers into CBS-TV City where we both were working and trying to figure out how she ever could pull up so much performing energy from such a tiny frame ...

Running often into Judy's husband and Liza's father Vincente Minnelli on the elevator at my shrink's office in Westwood and wondering if his problems were bigger than mine ...

Being honored by comedian Ken Murray asking me to appear in his "Hollywood Home Movies" while I was filming at Disney and thus joining the ranks of others he'd photographed in their off-moments like Chaplin, William Randolph Hearst and Marion Davies, Dietrich, Garbo, and Rin Tin Tin (woof!) ...

Wanting to call home during a break from a session at Gold Star Recording on Santa Monica Blvd., but unable to get through due to Cher's constantly yacking with her gal-pals and monopolizing the only available phone in the studio ...

Riding with a chatty Ginger Rogers in a hotel elevator and thinking how sad it was that Mr. Astaire's dancing partner was now confined to a wheelchair ...

Running into "Psycho" actor Tony Perkins at Blockbuster Video and feeling squeamish because in real life he seemed as spooky as Norman Bates ...

Delaying regular Wednesday-night invitation-only movie preview screenings at 20th Century Fox Studios until "the one ... the only" Groucho showed up: beret on head - cigar in hand - blonde on arm ...

But gradually things started to change – mostly in my own head. I began thinking more about tracing "Dead Germans" of the 18th century than I did about what movie or TV role was on the horizon. I got tired of never getting the girl in any script presented to me: in my heart I was Tom Cruise, but I had been pretty-well typecast as a nebbish and a wimp in most everything I did. I even started having trouble remembering my lines of dialogue, something that had never been a problem. It was as if The Universe was sending me a message – trying to tell me something.

As I wrote later in my book *Psychic Roots: Serendipity & Intuition in Genealogy:*

"My mid-life career crisis all seemed to crystalize and come to a head in the mid-1980s when I returned from giving a lecture in Salt Lake City at a conference of the National Genealogical Society. I must admit my talk had been well received, and I walked in the door of my home feeling terrific, thinking that perhaps I had contributed something of value to the genealogical community. After unwinding from the trip, I went to check my telephone answering machine for any important messages that might have been left in my absence. The only message on the tape was from my commercials agent, who urgently inquired, 'Can you be a dancing chicken at 3 o'clock?'

That did it. As much as I would have loved the nice residuals that my dancing chicken would have laid, I decided it was time to put away the grease paint (and feathers), move on, and concentrate fully on what had become my real love: genealogy!"

I've never regretted my decision. These days when I turn on the TV and see a rerun of one of my old shows it can get a bit spooky. Sometimes I'll be watching a particular scene and not know what I'm going to do next – even though it's me doing it. On other occasions I'll realize that the only person in a particular scene still living is yours truly: everybody else is dead! It can be rather surreal to be the "last man standing" at times.

People so often come up to me at genealogical gatherings and say, "My, what an interesting life you've led." It's true, and I'm *very* grateful. I guess I'm living proof of the old adage that says, "it's all about the journey, and the friends you meet along the way."

I've been SO blessed, and I appreciate it.

But what's next?

Bring it on!

MANUEL FELIX AT MUSSO & FRANK'S GRILL

MIMI WEBER & SOME OF HER CLIENTS AT HER BIRTHDAY PARTY

The WALT DISNEP Company.

Michael D. Eisner
Chairman of the Board and Chief Executive Officer

June 2, 1986

Mr. Hank Jones
4732 Placidia Avenue
Toluca Lake, CA 91602

Dear Hank:

Thank you for your very thoughtful letter on the passing
of Bob Stevensen.

Just about the first thing I did when I joined the company
was to enjoy a Disney film marathon, viewing the treasures
of the superb film library that is here. It became
quickly apparent that Bob made an enormous contribution to
the company's success and its reputation for quality
entertainment. In short, I couldn't agree with you more.

While the studio did issue a press release on his death,
I must acknowledge it was an unfortunate oversight not to
have run a memorial advertisement. However, since so much
time has passed it might appear to be an afterthought to
do so now and actually slight his memory.

Bob's great body of work will continue to be enjoyed by
future generations because of its quality and timelessness.
His memory will endure because of his rare talent.

Sincerely,

Michael D. Eisner
Chairman of the Board and
Chief Executive Officer

MDE:sm

LETTER FROM MICHAEL EISNER TO HANK JONES

IAN WOLFE
1896 - 1992

PERCY HELTON
1894 - 1971

CHARLES LANE
1905 -

DANA ANDREWS
1909 - 1992

Name Index

O'BRIEN
Parry, 138
Pat, 138
O'CONNELL
Arthur, 204
O'DAY
Anita, 225
O'FLAHERTY
Terrence, 44
O'HERLIHY
Michael, 149,
152-153, 213
O'NEAL
Kevin, 194
Ryan, 194
OBERON
Merle, 54
OLIVIER
Laurence, 8
ORBISON
Roy, 194
OSWALD, 109
Lee Harvey, 172
OWENS
Gary, 23
Jesse, 138
PALMER
Earl, 30
PANGBORN
Franklin, 119
PARKER
Butch, 89
Tom, 115
PARKS
Bert, 222
PARTON
Dolly, 199, 227
PASTERNAK
Joe, 115
PATTERSON
Bill, 76
PEARL
Minnie, 52, 59
PEARY
Harold, 176
PECK
Gregory, 80

PENN
Sean, 222
PERKINS
Roland, 198
Tony, 232
PETERS
Jon, 152
PHILLIPS
Sam, 26
PICKFORD
Mary, 79
PIDGEON
Walter, 229
PIKE
James, 114
PILKINGTON
Dave, 24, 107
Doris, 24, 107
PINE
Katie, 119
Robert, 119
PIOUS
Minerva, 119
PLESHETTE
Suzanne, 135,
139, 156
PLUMB
Eve, 28
Flora, 28
Neely, 25-29, 55,
58
PONS
Lily, 153
POOL
Mary Rose, 20
POPE JOHN PAUL II,
226
PORTER
Cole, 19
POTTER
Peter, 107
PREMINGER
Otto, 216-217
PRESLEY
Elvis, 20, 23, 26,
30, 115-117,
194, 227

PRESTON
Billy, 30
PRICE
Ben, 77
Lucille, 77
Vincent, 175
PRINCIPAL
Victoria, 172
PUMPIAN
Paul, 11-12, 77,
221
RADIN
Marion, 14
RAFT
George, 53
RAITT
Bonnie, 19
John, 19
RALKE
Don, 89
RAMSEY
Logan, 200
RANDALL
Ted, 23
RANNOW
Jerry, 118,
227-228, 230
Jewel Jaffe, 227
RAVEKES
John, 19
RAVENSCROFT
Thurl, 30
RAY
Eddie, 24
Larry [See Hayes,
Larry Ray],
Marlyne, 90
REESE
Della, 59
REID
Elliott, 137, 139
REINER
Carl, 150, 212
REITHERMAN
Woolie, 138
RENOUDET
Flo, 227